SCARRED FOR LIFE

ELEVEN STORIES ABOUT SKATEBOARDERS

BY KEITH DAVID HAMM

CHRONICLE BOOKS
SAN FRANCISCO

THIS BOOK IS DEDICATED TO MY FRIENDS:

TEAM AMATEUR,

FROM MY PAST,

AND THE

WILDERNESS BOWL BUILDERS,

FOREVER.

Text copyright ©2004 by KEITH DAVID HAMM

Library of Congress Cataloging-in-Publication Data available.

ISBN-13: 978-0-8118-4053-8

ISBN-10: 0-8118-4053-0

Manufactured in CHINA

Designed by ONE9INE

Distributed in Canada by RAINCOAST BOOKS

9050 SHAUGHNESSY STREET

VANCOUVER, BRITISH COLUMBIA V6P 6E5

10 9 8 7 6 5 4 3

CHRONICLE BOOKS LLC

85 SECOND STREET

SAN FRANCISCO, CA 94105
www.chroniclebooks.com

PAGE 1:
UNKNOWN SKATER, OLLIE, DOWNTOWN SANTA BARBARA, 1989
PHOTO: CHRISTOPHER GARDNER

PAGE 2:
JEN O'BRIEN, FRONTSIDE AIR AT THE HOME OFFICE, VISTA, CALIFORNIA, SPRING 2003
PHOTO: DÉSIRÉE ASTORGA

PAGES 6–7:
DITCH RUN, NEW MEXICO, APRIL 2003
PHOTO: RHINO

PAGES 8–9:
BUCKY LASEK, BACKSIDE AIR, VISTA, CALIFORNIA, APRIL 2003
PHOTO: DÉSIRÉE ASTORGA

ACKNOWLEDGMENTS

FOR EACH PERSON WHO COPPED AN ATTITUDE, there were dozens more who helped me out, and for their time and encouragement, I am grateful.

By providing me with food, clothing, warm places to sleep, quiet places to write, and odd jobs during thin times, each member of my immediate family helped this book happen. Thank you all.

Out on the road, I spent many nights, as planned, in the back of my truck. Other nights, cool people—from Hawaii to Canada to New York—put me up. Thanks, everybody. And if you're ever in my neck and need a place to crash, the back of my truck's always open.

For one or more of the following—invaluable input and feedback, kicks in the ass, extraordinary photo roundups, high-tech assistance, and guidance to stones in need of turning—I thank Pete Connelly, Kent Dahlgren, Darrel Delgado, Robert Feigel, Glen E. Friedman, Jason Jessee, Davoud Kermaninejad at *Concussion*, Justin McIvor at MG Imaging, Coan Nichols at NCP Films, Julie Oxendale, Chris Rooney, Bret Taylor, Jean Yamamura, and especially Jim Knight. My firstborn will be divided equally among you.

Last, I'd like to lay it on thick for my agent, Diana Finch, who believed in the book from the get; for my editor, Alan Rapp, who trusted me; and designers Azi Rad and Warren Corbitt, who made it look good.

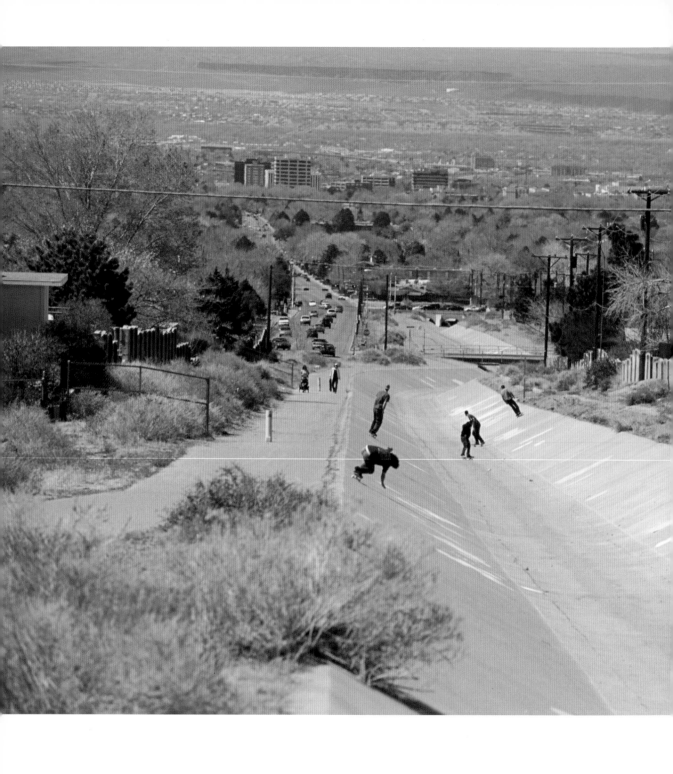

CONTENTS

INTRODUCTION

Must have been a drought year. Because in the late winter of 1977, when my hometown on the outskirts of Santa Cruz should have been drenched by weeks of rain, my two older brothers dug a huge hole in my sisters' garden, lined it with chicken wire, and poured concrete into it. They laid down the final trowel-swipes on March 8 and pressed beer-bottle caps into the tacky concrete, and the next afternoon, while the surface was still green in a few places, the session was on. The Bowl was born.

About eighteen feet in diameter and maybe five feet at its deepest point, the Bowl was shaped like a keyhole. It had a rounded lip all around, and one side pitched up almost vertically. Sheets of plywood fed into the shallow section, down which my brothers and their friends pushed at high speed before carving through the so-called deep end.

This is where I first learned to skateboard. I was six. I remember Ted Nugent, UFO, Led Zeppelin, and Black Sabbath blasting from the boom box. Hang Ten shorts and big hair. Skinny skateboards and no pads. But I had no idea that skateboarding was a national craze or that concrete skateparks were cropping up across the States and beyond. I knew nothing about the roots of skateboarding, laid down by Southern California surfers in the late '50s and early '60s, maybe even longer ago. In fact, it's part of the public record that a San Diego surf grommet intentionally nailed together the first bona fide "skateboard" in the summer of 1947. But that story, like much of skateboard lore, is a truth based on withered memories and lost facts. Anyway, when I was six years old, I could've cared less. I just wanted some fun. And thanks to that drought and my obsessed brothers, I got some.

THE FIRST TIME I STEPPED ON A SKATEBOARD, I stood with my left foot on the tail, which made me a goofy-footer.

That lasted about ten seconds. My brothers, both regular-footers, made me switch. They taught me to push off, coast straight into the Bowl, and ride up the opposite wall and straight back down again, without turning. That's called a fakie. (More lore: It's been said that Jay Adams—one of the most spontaneous and innovative skateboarders of his day—invented the fakie in some bone-dry backyard swimming pool in the mid-'70s. You see, Jay was *supposed* to ride up the wall, turn around, and come back down, but instead he just rode straight up and came right back down backward, faking out everybody who was watching.) I also learned backside kick-turns (180-degree pivots, back to the lip) and frontside kick-turns (same thing, except facing the lip), flowing and flailing about halfway up the wall. Sometimes my brothers built towering plywood extensions jutting skyward from the lip of the Bowl. I couldn't even sniff those.

Early on, I didn't skate that often. Mainly because I had nobody my age to skate with. Besides, I was more into soccer, baseball, and getting loose on my BMX bike. One of my brothers, however, did shape me a deck in woodshop class, completing it with some hand-me-down trucks and urethane wheels. I rode it sometimes in the Bowl with the big guys and sometimes on rainy days, tick-tacking circles around the garage until I was dizzy, then circling the other way, thinking I could get un-dizzy. As skateboarding's widespread popularity dried up more or less around 1980—as all but a handful of skateparks closed, mainly because of skyrocketing insurance premiums—and my brothers graduated from high school and moved out, I stopped skating. The Bowl filled with rainwater.

But in the late summer of 1984, I started seeing skateboarders my age cruising around the playground before school each morning. They just stepped off the bus, boards in hand, and started riding. No coaches to tell them how to do it. No uniforms to brand them as a team. No rulebooks to keep them in line. I wanted in. And this time it was for good. I quit everything: soccer, baseball, BMX, and a brief and supremely frustrating stint with golf. I bought a new board, subscribed to *Thrasher*, built ramps, found empty pools, swept out drainage ditches, skated empty parking lots alone in the middle of the night, and, of course, drained the Bowl.

Skateboarding was it. But it's hard to explain why. It was fun, yeah, but there's something else. It got in my blood. The freedom. The flow. The wind in my face. Smooth swerves. Speed carves. Good pain and bad pain. Innovation and adaptation. Limitless terrain. Punk rock. The absence of rules. The unknown rippers. The new friends for life. Riding attached but not attached to this piece of wood with four wheels, I found skateboarding to be both transportation and expression, and it made me brave and creative at the same time. What more does a young man need?

Even today, as the Xtreme ActionSport Formerly Known as Skateboarding dominates the airwaves— packaged, marketed, pawned off to consumers of "alternative culture"—its roots can still be found. In fact, during the past couple years, especially since that *Dogtown and Z-Boys* documentary, a lot of skateboarders, mostly the older set, have been revisiting history, drunk with nostalgia, some going as far as to collect any and all skateboard paraphernalia in any condition and sell it for big bucks on the Internet. *If I had only kept my old decks instead of burning them at our summer beach bonfires . . .*

THIS BOOK WAS BLESSED by injury. If I hadn't busted my ankle in the Vans combi-pool in May 2002 (rolled it after sketching out on a 50-50 through the corner), I wouldn't have sat on my ass—left leg encased in plaster and propped on my desk—for seven weeks doing nothing except reading, interviewing, and writing about skateboarding. If I hadn't been weak from that flimsy ankle for many more moons, I would have spent my summer in the Pacific Northwest, skating the best skateparks on the planet, instead of tracking down the men who built them and getting them to talk about it. If I hadn't popped my right knee in June 2003 (fluked a rock-and-roll in an empty Santa Monica swimming pool and ended up doing the James Brown soul splits at high speed), I wouldn't have holed up at my desk once again, typing the final chapters and this introduction and incessantly hounding photographers to submit their images before deadline.

The ironic timing of my injuries struck me as strange, really. I'd get a good interview with some elusive skateboarder I'd been stalking for months, or I'd come across generous photographers with great images, or I'd write something halfway decent about this way of life, to which I felt I could hardly do justice because I was too close to it, and then I'd get all fired up and go skateboarding. And I'd keep on skateboarding, putting off important phone calls, blowing off another afternoon of writing at the Central Library in downtown L.A., and fooling myself: "Oh, I'm conducting hands-on research right now, grinding this backyard bowl with my friends." And then I'd slam— very hard—break something, shake my head, and get back to work. It was as if skateboarding itself, somehow, was shaking me by the shoulders, yelling, "You gotta get off your damn board and finish that book!"

So here it is. Enjoy. I'll be skateboarding.

1

HILLS

SPEED FREAKS)

CLIFF COLEMAN WAS THE FIRST MAN ON THE SCENE

THAT DAY IN MCLAREN PARK WHEN BUTT-BOARDER ERIC KEEPO'O SLAMMED FEET FIRST INTO A HAY BALE AT FORTY

PREVIOUS:
CLIFF COLEMAN DOES A BOARD-TO-BOARD JUMP, SPROUL PLAZA, UC BERKELEY, 1965
PHOTO: JOE LUCERO, COURTESY OF CLIFF COLEMAN

NEXT:
BURNING DOWN THE NARROW STRAIGHTS OF BUENA VISTA ROAD IN EXCESS OF FORTY MILES AN HOUR, JIM CLUGGISH (LEFT) AND CLIFF COLEMAN SLIDE BACKWARD THROUGH A TIGHT TURN IN THE BERKELEY HILLS, MAY 2000.
PHOTO: MICHAEL BREAM

MILES PER HOUR. Watching the race from turn two, a steep and sweeping ninety-degree left-hander, the fastest section of the course, Coleman had seen the crash coming. The wide, smooth asphalt road was still damp in large, dark patches, like conspicuous land mines laid by the last three days of heavy rain, spring 2001's first downpour for San Francisco. Decked out in a full-face helmet and black racing leathers and reclined on his over-sized skateboard, Keepo'o had rocketed through the wet and the dry and leaned into turn two, hugging a tight line. And he was looking good. Until the wobble. As he lost control for an instant in a rain slick, a slight side-to-side speed shimmy pitched Keepo'o off his line, and his back wheels slid out just enough to send him straight for the hay. A few long, terribly long seconds later, he drove like a nail into that storm-soaked bale, pushing it back a solid seven feet before sliding from his board at the course's edge, in agony, clasping his lower right leg with both hands.

Broken tibia. Three places. Compound fracture.

While most spectators winced, stared, and gasped, Coleman rushed to Keepo'o's side as the first signs of blood seeped between his fingers and dripped to the cold road. "Gruesome," Coleman thought. But he didn't say it. Better for Keepo'o—now on the verge of slipping into deep shock and quietly ranting to nobody in particular, "Oh, no . . . this isn't good, this isn't good"—to hear something more soothing. "Take a couple deep breaths and try and relax," Coleman told him calmly. "Help is on the way." By the time the ambulance arrived, Keepo'o had settled down some-what into a shrug-shouldered capitulation to the unavoidable consequences of riding down a steep hill on a skateboard—a simple, four-wheeled tool built for speed and maneuverability that, by design and since its inception, has never had brakes. The para-medics hauled out a stretcher, neck brace, and first-aid kit. Leaning over the crooked limb and brandishing a pair of scissors, the paramedic in charge asked Keepo'o, "How much do you like these leathers?"

Keepo'o was quickly stabilized on a stretcher and hauled off toward the hospital. By then, many of the rain slicks had evaporated under the day's dim sun-shine, and racing had resumed, a competition of con-temporary classes, from luge and "classic luge" (also known as butt-boarding or butt-bombing) to gravity bikes and in-line skates. None of these offshoots really interested Coleman. He was waiting for the day's main event: the stand-up skateboarding finals. This was the style of riding in which Coleman, then fifty-two, was born and bred, the pure and simple act of standing on a skateboard and letting gravity take over, the original genre that had consumed Coleman's existence for more than four decades.

As so many dedicated skateboarders eventually realize, skateboarding becomes much more than an exhilarating, challenging pastime. For Coleman,

skateboarding has taken on several meanings over the years. From day one, skateboarding has been something fun to do. But it has also fueled and cooled his competitive nature. It's been his mantra, his therapist, his outlet for grace and aggression. A path to goals and desires. A source of freedom and creativity. A crime, a drug, a passion, a job, a gift to give and receive. Skateboarding is pleasure, pain, sweat, blood, and scar tissue. A debilitating slam and a fountain of youth. A barking grind, a soothing hum, a blur of road seen through tear-streaked eyes. A bridge to another world filled with friends who are like family. An understatement, an exaggeration. And, of course, a great story.

THE STORY OF COLEMAN'S LIFELONG addiction to skateboarding is a tour of terrain. Like all skateboarders, Coleman has his "spots," those familiar places where he is most comfortable on his board, where confidence and style conspire to shatter boundaries and craft new traditions. Many skaters have a favorite marble ledge or staircase handrail. Others find their creative freedom on towering half-pipes. A few get off carving empty backyard swimming pools. Coleman's spots run through the hills of California's East Bay. "Back in '65, there was no ramp skating or pool skating," Coleman says. "It was who had the best hills. Hills were the thing. And some of us still know that."

Born on November 22, 1949, in Hawaii and raised as a Navy brat, following his father from Honolulu to Memphis, San Diego, and Yokohama, Coleman, at the age of seven, finally dropped anchor with his mother, older brother, and younger sister in the Berkeley Hills. Young and athletic, Coleman lived near the top of steep and snaking Buena Vista Road,

IN 1965 THE HOBIE VITA PAKT SUPER SURFER SKATEBOARD TEAM RECRUITED BERKELEY STANDOUT DANNY ESCALANTE (RIGHT) FOR A NATIONAL TOUR. ALSO PICTURED, FROM LEFT TO RIGHT, ARE DANNY BEARER, DAVE HILTON, AND JOHN FREIS PHOTO COURTESY OF DANIEL BEARER

I'M NOT GOING TO RACE A BUTT-BOARD—EVER. I'M NOT GOING TO RIDE A LUGE—EVER. BUT WHEN YOU'VE GOT A GROUP OF LUGE GUYS COMING DOWN THE HILL INCHES APART AND THE HILL'S GOT SOME TURNS TO MAKE IT INTERESTING, IT'S EXCITING. BUT, NO, A LUGE IS NOT A SKATEBOARD. IF ALL THEY DO IS LUGE, IF THEY DON'T STAND UP, NO, THEY'RE NOT SKATEBOARDERS
CLIFF COLEMAN

where the dramatic topography dictated the form of his fun. Before he'd even heard of a skateboard, Coleman was barreling down Buena Vista in a red wagon, racing his neighborhood cohorts. They also nailed roller skates to a broken door, pointed the slapdash contraption downhill, and jumped on it, three or four at a time, staying on until it inevitably veered into the bushes or one of the steel wheels seized against an acorn, flinging the laughing boys against the asphalt. Off-road, they launched mountainous jumps on their BMX bikes and rode sheets of cardboard down grassy hillsides.

Coleman's first skateboard was a gift from a member of UC Berkeley's rowing crew, an older group he

CLIFF COLEMAN, SIERRA WAVE SKATEPARK, SACRAMENTO, CALIFORNIA, 1978
PHOTO COURTESY OF CLIFF COLEMAN

hung with frequently and who partially filled the void left by his father's departure. A rattling death-trap typical of the time, the board was two sets of steel wheels from a dismantled roller skate nailed to a short length of two-by-four. Coleman stepped on and—as with most people when they first try skate-boarding—wham! He fell on his ass. It hurt. But he was eleven, so he tried again. And, with a kid's knack for learning quickly, Coleman soon got the hang of it.

Within a year or so, Coleman had upgraded his steel-wheeled two-by-four to a Makaha skateboard with Chicago-brand trucks (the pivoting hangers on which the wheels spin) and clay wheels, and he had come down from the familiar hills to ride with the older kids on the Berkeley campus, a rolling play-ground of smooth asphalt paths and parking garages. Shadowing the best riders, mainly Berkeley standout Danny Escalante, Coleman mastered the basics: popping nose-wheelies while hanging ten toes off the front of his board like a landlocked surfer; stalling long, rolling handstands; and lifting his front wheels and spinning 360-degree revolutions. Their "skate-board craze" antics were soon exposed by the *San Francisco Chronicle* and the now-defunct *Berkeley*

Gazette, and Coleman and crew landed a sponsor.

"In December 1964," Coleman remembers, "the Hobie skateboard team came up to do a [demonstration] at the Cow Palace at the San Francisco Sport and Boat Show. Let's see . . . the Hobie guys were George Trafton, Torger Johnson, Danny Bearer, Wendy Bearer, Colleen Boyd, the Hilton brothers. I'm probably leaving somebody out. Anyway, the organizers of the show had read about us in the paper and hired us to ride alongside the Hobie team. Dave Rochlen was their manager, and he looked at us as the Northern California skateboard talent pool, equal to his southern crew."

By 1965 Coleman was touring with Hobie's Northern California Team. Back then, landing a "sponsor" meant, much as it does now, free stuff. Hobie flowed Coleman skateboards (the twenty-seven-inch pressed-fiberglass "spoon" was *the* board of choice), a custom surfboard (a nine-foot, three-inch-long, nineteen-and-a-half-inch-wide Phil Edwards design with three redwood stringers), and clothes (Levis, low-top deck shoes made by Vans precursor Randolph Rubber Company, and a navy-blue jacket embossed with the Hobie "Super Surfer Skateboard Team" logo), and it paid for weekend road trips to demonstrations (or "demos") and contests. Competing in the downhill slalom division, Coleman beat out hundreds of skaters on his way to nineteenth place at skateboarding's first world championships, held in May 1965 in Anaheim, California.

One day that same year, Coleman and a few of his buddies were hanging out in a UC Berkeley parking garage, practicing what they called one-footed power slides. In a move similar to what he did in the dirt on his BMX bike, Coleman worked up speed across the garage, planted his front foot on the smooth concrete, and with his back foot pushed the tail of his skateboard into a screeching slide. Loud and fun, to be sure, but removing a foot from the board was kind of cheating. Coleman remembers thinking, "Gee, if

I'M NOT INTERESTED IN IN-LINING OR LUGING OR GRAVITY BIKES, THAT KIND OF STUFF, BUT I REALIZE THAT THERE ARE ALL THESE DIVERSE INTERESTS IN LEISURE-TIME ACTIVITIES BASED ON GRAVITY, AND IT'S JUST A NATURAL THING FOR GUYS TO BECOME INTERESTED IN THEM. THOSE THINGS DON'T DRAW MY INTEREST, BUT I HAVE AN APPRECIATION FOR THEM. BUT YOU HAVE TO REMEMBER: THEY'RE ALL DERIVATIVES OF SKATEBOARDING
JOHN HUTSON

we could only do those slides with both feet on." A decade passed, and during it skateboarding's popularity fell and rose again before Coleman witnessed a maneuver similar to what he and his friends had dreamed about in that parking garage.

Between 1965 and 1975, Coleman, six foot one and in peak physical condition, strayed from skateboarding, expressing himself in high school as a diver and later studying tae kwon do. He boxed through a brief stint in college and took to scaling the Yosemite Valley's granite monoliths alongside climbing great Peter Haan during the late '60s and early '70s. He

kept his hair long, never smoked (cigarettes, anyway), and avoided alcohol because it hit him like poison. At the time, Berkeley was a hotbed of antiwar activism, but what helped Coleman to stay clear of the killing fields of Vietnam was his long battle with recurring migraines. Shortly after registering for the draft, Coleman was given 1A (draft-eligible) status, which was later downgraded because of his debilitating headaches. One year later, an army doctor prescribed Coleman pain preventatives and reinstated his 1A status. Coleman was drafted but refused his induction. He was indicted, convicted, and sentenced to eighteen months in federal prison, and his last hope rested with an appeal to the Ninth Circuit Court, where it was found that his 1A status had been unlawfully bestowed. Coleman, exonerated, didn't spend one day in jail, or at war. With a woman he loved and thoughts of a family, Coleman married in 1972.

By the mid-'70s, Frank Nashworthy's polyurethane wheel had single-handedly instigated skateboarding's second wave. The difference between the smooth-rolling, road-hugging urethane wheels and the rock-hard, bone-rattling ride of clay wheels was night and day, a dramatic change much like Coleman's childhood upgrade from steel to clay wheels. With a new Black Knight board his mom had bought him, Coleman dove back into skateboarding.

When he wasn't spending time with his wife or working as a Bay Area truck driver, Coleman was skating. In 1975, during the Northern California Skateboard Championships, skate great Torger Johnson, a holdover from the '60s boom, leaned on the nose of his board as a pivot point, then slid the tail 180 degrees without removing either foot from the board. Johnson's maneuver was part pivot, part slide, and when Coleman saw it, the parking-garage memories of those one-footed power slides came rushing back. Inspired, he took to the hills of

BOTH ARMS BACK INSTEAD OF PIERCING STRAIGHT AHEAD,
JOHN HUTSON (PICTURED LEFT AND ABOVE) TAKES
A QUALIFYING RUN ON SEPTEMBER 3, 1983, AT THE CAPITOLA CLASSIC.
HUTSON INTRODUCED HIS STREAMLINED "HUT TUCK" TO COMPETITIVE
DOWNHILLERS IN THE '70S, AND THAT'S HOW PRETTY MUCH EVERYBODY HAS
RACED EVER SINCE
PHOTOS COURTESY OF JOHN HUTSON

Orinda, just outside Berkeley, where he worked up a bit of downhill speed, crouched to lower his center of gravity, and, rolling his rear knee forward, shifted his body weight over his front wheels, causing his back wheels to break free and slide around. This experimental downhill slide was the seed of the innovations that would eventually enable Coleman to stand-up skate twisting streets of any steepness, in control and holding his own lane—pushing speeds in excess of fifty miles per hour.

Mapped out in his mind like a desiccated ski resort, the matrix of roads in the Berkeley Hills served as a perfect playground on which Coleman could hone his slide. One plunge, the Buena Vista Run, snaking through Coleman's old neighborhood, is a linkage of streets winding nearly two miles and kinked with fifteen hairpin turns. With its narrow, tight switchbacks, simply driving up it in an automobile demands focused attention. Bombing down it on a skateboard, however, requires something more. Call it insanity. It's steep and narrow and windy, with cars and trucks and motorcycles coming up and going down and parked all along it. Rough manhole covers and jutting road reflectors and gravel and twigs and branches litter both lanes. Dogs lunge barking from hidden yards. And every driveway spilling onto Buena Vista is Russian roulette—a potentially lethal chamber loaded with a vehicle on the move. Buena Vista was Coleman's favorite run. Still is.

Downhill skateboarding, which led Coleman and

company to the highest and most tortuous routes in the Berkeley Hills, progressed in large part because of its illicitness. Every time the cops booted the boys from their favorite downhilling spot, they sought out steeper, more remote terrain. Pushed by police and campus authorities, Coleman and his friends went from the university's inclines and parking garages in the '60s to Old Tunnel Road and its tributaries from '75 to '77, where Coleman first experimented with downhill sliding and they all polished drafting techniques along the lengthy, gently sloped runs. After getting kicked off Tunnel, the boys went back to UC Berkeley, and for a short spell, on weekends mostly, lounged in the shade near the North Gate and smoked sticky green marijuana before racing down what they called Seismograph Hill or simply "Seismo," a short, sweet drop from the Earth Sciences building to the library. That didn't last long, however, and, in 1978, campus police pushed them once again. "Find some other spot to ride those things" was the standard spiel. Coleman ran for the hills.

While Berkeley's police officers and campus cops had inadvertently helped to advance the area's downhill scene by pushing skaters into the steeper hills, the skaters' most massive progress unfolded while they were hot on the tail of an insanely fast downhiller named Noel McComas. If Coleman and the rest were the greyhounds, McComas was the rabbit—always faster, always just out of reach. McComas had grown up skiing the Sierra Nevadas, the kind of skier whose runs always started from the resorts' highest peaks and dropped full speed back to the lift line, as fast as he could and without stopping. He'd do this until the lifts shut down for the night. On the dry roads of Oakland as a boy, he'd ride long wheelies down the street on his ten-speed. He'd cruise his Fiberflex skateboard with a tightened, forward-pointing stance, as if he was parallel skiing, searching for the speed he found on the snowy mountains. When he got his license, he was an instant type-A driver. For McComas, adrenaline addiction had come early in life, and the point of no return occurred when the speed of skiing and the feel of soft urethane on smooth asphalt meshed unforgettably—the day he pulled on a pair of roller skates.

Long ago, kids invented skateboarding by ripping apart roller skates, an act of destruction and creation that foreshadowed the pure and proud independence and innovation that would later characterize the culture. And to witness a roller-skater rolling with a pack of downhill skateboarders was rare and odd, if not entirely unique. Like a Vespa mod rallying with Hell's Angels, it just didn't seem right. But for Coleman and the rest, McComas's choice of transportation was a nonissue. Boiled down, the Berkeley scene, it seemed, was all about speed. Coleman recalls: "I've really gone after him, you know, tucking through the straightaways, really chasing him, and I've only passed Noel once in twenty-five years. One time. And he was probably daydreaming. Noel pushed us as skateboarders to a whole new level just because he was so much faster than us. And I don't care what he's ridin', as long as we're out there going fast and having a good time."

COLEMAN AND HIS CASTAWAYS honed their slides and increased their velocity down the Berkeley Hills network of what has been estimated at—counting all the crossroad combinations—more than a hundred runs. But he also branched out from his home hills to enter speed contests. Standing out in his memory, an accident-plagued race day in the summer of 1978 outside Long Beach, California, marked the so-called Death of Downhill. Hundreds of onlookers and a

THE MOST FLASHY AND SOLID OF THE NEW GENERATION, BRAZILIAN SERGIO YUPPIE IS ONE OF THE WORLD'S BEST DOWNHILL SLIDERS. PICTURED HERE IN DEL MAR, CALIFORNIA, YUPPIE STANDS A NOSE-WHEELIE SLIDE AT HIGH SPEED, FALL 2002
PHOTO: MICHAEL BREAM

handful of reporters from *Sports Illustrated* and local television news stations witnessed no fewer than a dozen people—even fellow spectators—injured, one critically. The big problem arose from many of the participants in the modified division, a category welcoming customized "skatecars," fully enclosed aerodynamic experiments that looked more like lowrider rocket ships than accessorized skateboards. Writing for *Skateboarder* magazine, Brian Gillogly explained, "This year's race was not a professional-class event. In fact, some of the participants . . . proved no less than rank amateurs, fool-hardily braving the infamous drop in untried—and often unworkable—vehicles." In the stand-up event, however, racing unfolded with few mishaps. Coleman, then sponsored by Santa Cruz Skateboards, landed fourth place, behind Hobie's Bob Skolberg, and second-place Michael Goldman, who also rode for Santa Cruz, which at the time dominated the world of competitive downhilling. The day's top trophy went to another Santa Cruz rider, John Hutson, arguably the world's best competitive downhiller, a talent Coleman, to this day, considers "the greatest racer of all time, miles ahead of second place."

Hutson remembers that day on Signal Hill as both a boon and a blow to downhilling. Mainstream interest in skateboarding was peaking at that point, and the event seemed as much a promotional gimmick as it did a bonafide competition, the former drawing novice riders—some of them celebrities from other alternative thrill rides, such as hang-gliding—who climbed into experimental skatecars. The resulting crash-and-burn spectacle overshadowed Hutson's 53.45-mile-per-hour first-place run, which put him into the *Guinness Book of World Records*, a record he held for more than a decade.

For years to come, Coleman remembers, sanction-

SKATEBOARDING HAS ALWAYS BEEN A WAY OF GETTING BY IN CALIFORNIA. IT ALWAYS PROVIDED ME WITH FRIENDS, JOBS, FLOORS TO CRASH ON. DO A LITTLE SIGHTSEEING, SKATE SOME NEW HILLS. I LOVE SKATING. I THINK ABOUT IT WHEN I'M NOT DOING IT. I CARE ABOUT IT. I CARE ABOUT GOING FASTER, CUTTING A CORNER A LITTLE SHARPER. I'M A LITTLE OBSESSED WITH IT . . . AND I LIKE IT EVEN MORE WHEN IT'S NOT POPULAR. THE FREEDOM, THE CULT NATURE, THE UNDERGROUND STATUS, SKATERS DOING IT FOR FUN AND THERE'S NO PHOTOGRAPHER AROUND—THAT'S THE ESSENCE OF IT FOR ME, THE TRUE HEART AND SOUL
JIM CLUGGISH

ing bodies had a difficult time securing race permits. With a few reappearances, most memorably at Laguna Seca automotive speedway and during the Capitola Classic, both in Central California, the competitive scene slowly faded. Many racers gave up on skateboarding; others simply returned to their hometown spots, trailing pace cars and clocking times that unofficially hammered Hutson's world record. (Hutson, too, was breaking sixty miles per hour down his training hill, Rampart Road, a two-lane frontage paralleling Highway 1 through Watsonville, California.)

Yet back in the hills of Berkeley, downhilling thrived. Coleman discovered he could prolong and better control his slides—and, therefore, attack hills with greater speed—by shifting a considerable portion of his body weight to his leading, gloved hand as he dragged it along the pavement behind his sideways-sliding board. Leather gloves, however, skimmed the asphalt with too much friction and quickly burned through. So, to the palms of their gloves they glued thin, hard-plastic objects—road reflectors worked well, as did "skid plates" or "tail bones," originally designed to shield the underside of a skateboard's tail from excessive wear. They also salvaged high-density scraps from Bay Area plastic factories. With these specialized gloves, the downhill slide really took form—an innovative, safe, and exceedingly stylish method of slowing down. Now they could build up as much speed as they wanted through the straightaways and, as the turns approached, drop into a slide, distributing their very low center of gravity between their sliding wheels and dragging hand. Then they could swing their boards forward and back like a pendulum, scrubbing away speed the whole time, before standing again in the next stretch of acceleration. Many variations on this standard pendulum slide (sometimes called the Coleman Slide) arose as the downhillers slid in and out of corners going backward or dropped forward onto both plastic-lined palms, burning around corners with their backs to the sky before wrapping the slide around 360 degrees.

Brian Lilla best captured the elegant insanity of their runs in his 2002 Super-8 skateboard film, *Twenty to Life*. Jim Cluggish, then thirty-eight, narrated its downhilling segment. As the black-and-white footage captures him roadside, brandishing a board with wheels torn to tatters by the day's runs, he recalls his first time. "The neighbors across the street had a skateboard, a wooden skateboard with clay wheels, and all the little bearings would come out of the wheels, a long time ago." Then the film cuts to him approaching forty miles per hour down Buena Vista, leaning through a left-handed hairpin at the intersection of Campus and Del Mar, sliding off just enough speed to make it through the corner, in complete control, grazing a wide crack between the road and the shoulder and just missing a parked car before standing again and rocketing down the next straightaway. "And I remember the day when I could go from the top of their driveway to the bottom of their driveway without falling off. I was maybe eight years old."

BORN ON JANUARY 4, 1964, Cluggish was raised in Wellesley, Massachusetts, and lived on the East Coast until he boarded a one-way flight to San Francisco on September 5, 1982. He had just graduated from high school and the thought of another bitter Northeast winter drove him to the temperate West, where colleges were relatively inexpensive and skateboarders rode year-round. His memory: "It was unusual back east to be a hardcore skater. But when I came to California, it was almost a necessity." Through skateboarding, Cluggish found friends, jobs, and a place to hang his hat. Many East Bay skaters lived in a large house at the bottom of Strawberry Canyon, renting rooms from a highly intelligent, free-basing homosexual doctor with a very young boyfriend. Semicreepy landlord notwithstanding, the house served as a meeting point for downhillers (such as Chris Pettyjohn, Mark Aley, Caedmon Bear, and a handful of roller-skaters, among others), who caught the Humphrey GoBart free shuttle from downtown Berkeley to the

Lawrence Hall of Science, then cut through a yard to the top of Grizzly Peak, the starting point of a long run back to the lowlands. "We'd start up in the cold fog and end up down with the pretty girls on campus," remembers Cluggish. "A magic-carpet ride through the neighborhoods," tucking and carving through the straights and sliding through the corners, always mindful of their lane and heeding the signals—single-arm windmill for "go," both arms up for "stop"—from lookouts posted on blind corners.

Cluggish and Coleman became friends instantly, and in the fall of 1983 they traveled to Santa Barbara to put on a semisecret downhill meet in the hills of Montecito. No sponsors, no hype, no trophies. Coleman's back-hills "contest" was the type of competition that Cluggish could stomach, and he ended up placing sixth out of a grand total of eight skaters. "Organization is counter to skateboarding," Cluggish explains. "Skating was always a way for me to *not* be part of an organization. Once you start competing, you know, you have to get up early on the weekends and pay money and start your run at point A and end it at point B and sometimes skate a hill you don't want to skate. It's not my thing."

Landing a sanding job at Powell-Peralta Skateboards, Cluggish stayed in Santa Barbara, slid his college aspirations to the back burner, and skated the region's ditches, reservoirs, and backyard pools with his new family of skaters, namely Chris Iverson, Chuck Barfoot, Evan Feen, and others. After a year of sucking sawdust in the Powell-Peralta sanding room, Cluggish quit to pursue a massage credential, which sent him to a Jamaican resort for six months. Back in Santa Barbara, he quit massage and worked at a handful of surf/skate shops until he applied to universities in the early '90s. By the fall of 1993, he was back in Berkeley, earning a bachelor's of science degree in chemistry from the university and taking hill runs again with Coleman and the rest. Since Coleman seemed to know pretty much everybody in town, hitching rides to Grizzly Peak proved easy. Sometimes, they'd ride the number 8 or 65 buses. For $1.50 and a transfer, they could get in six runs, sliding the turns all weekend, burning through wheels until they had none left. On Monday morning, Coleman would phone his countless connections, and within a few days boxes of new wheels would show up on his doorstep.

By the time Cluggish returned to the clan of Berkeley downhillers, the recent high points of Coleman's life had somewhat balanced a deep low: he had lost his estranged wife to a fatal fight with alcohol and witnessed his teenage son and young daughter suffer the loss of their mother. Those who know him best suggest that Coleman didn't dwell on a painful past or worry about an unpredictable future—he simply carried on, his nearly Zen-like devotion to the present at last replacing tragedy with fortuity. Not only had Coleman become California's three-time yo-yo champion, he bagged the national title in 1994. He moved on to judging yo-yo competitions worldwide, pocketing more money than he had ever earned skateboarding. From 1996 to 2000, he managed a small team of yo-yo masters, organizing demonstrations in Hawaii, Vegas, Chicago, the five boroughs of New York, Europe, Japan, and Australia. (He later tapped his frequent-flyer miles for a ticket to race downhill in Austria.)

Without embarrassment, Coleman concedes that he invented virtually all of his title-winning, groundbreaking yo-yo trick combinations while lucidly inebriated on high-grade Northern California marijuana. Smoking pot had always been part of the downhilling scene as well, part of the sensory thrill and focused confidence and therapeutic catharsis of approaching hairpin turns at forty-five miles per hour. Coleman's conviction: "If you're in a bad relationship or your job's not working out, you can come up here and smoke a fat one with your friends and share a great view of the Golden Gate Bridge and go skateboarding. Your troubles fade."

CLIFF COLEMAN, BERKELEY HILLS, CIRCA 1980
PHOTO COURTESY OF CLIFF COLEMAN

BACK IN THE HILLS of San Francisco's McLaren Park, Coleman propped his elbows on a double stack of hay bales on the outside edge of turn two, where Keepo'o had buckled his leg. His old friend Noel McComas stood nearby. Cupping his hands against his salt-and-pepper beard, Coleman screamed encouragement to Patrick Rizzo, eighteen, who blazed by in good form, on his way to bagging the tallest trophy in the stand-up skateboarding event, his first win. Rizzo's close friend Joseph "JM" Duran, also eighteen, would place fifth, and later both would credit Coleman as their mentor. "He took us under his wing," Duran says.

"He taught us the Berkeley style first—you know, all the slides—then turned us on to the racing scene."

If it wasn't for his lack of medical insurance and his slow push-starts caused by his bum ankle—chronically weak from a bathroom slip sustained in 1998 during a yo-yo tour through Korea—Coleman would have been racing against his protégés that day. Old enough to remember when uninsured skaters could risk spectacular injury chasing trophies, Coleman considers competition a given of the lifestyle, but at the same time, he has survived without it when skateboarding's popularity dropped, forcing competitive racers back to the hills where they were born.

Coleman gazed east toward his Berkeley Hills, then turned to McComas.

"Hey, Noel," he said. "Let's get out of here before they ask us to help load up these hay bales."

2 THE '60s
ROOTS

ON
JULY 3,
1964,
A YOUNG SURFER NAMED
JIM FITZPATRICK
BOARDED AN AIRPLANE
IDLING ON THE TARMAC
AT LOS ANGELES
INTERNATIONAL

AIRPORT.

Set off by his sun-bleached hair and bronzed body, his blue eyes sparkled with anticipation. The plane, chartered by the United States Surfing Association and *Surfguide* magazine, was bound for Paris, where Fitzpatrick would catch a ride to the French coastal town Biarritz, the heart of Europe's inchoate surf scene. Fitzpatrick, accompa-nied by his uncle, found his seat and waited for the liftoff of the European Surfing Holiday, a five-week safari of a lifetime for the sixteen-year-old surfer.

Advertised in *Surfguide*, the European Surfing Holiday offered roundtrip airfare, a train to the coast, and five nights in a Biarritz hotel for four hundred dol-lars. Anyone was welcome, and Fitzpatrick's fellow passengers included surfers, travelers, and a few retired couples drawn to the bargain price. Not all of the two hundred available seats were filled, and the trip's frontman, Larry Kraus, a mathematical analyst for the Rand Corporation who would later ditch that job for a thirty-one-year stint as an L.A. County lifeguard, scrambled to sell off the remaining seats at one hun-dred bucks a pop. Full-price payers caught wind of the liquidation and wanted compensation. Others demanded full refunds when they laid eyes on the air-craft: The underpaid airline had downgraded its initial jet-engine offer to a rattling prop plane. Fitzpatrick could have cared less—it would be a long and teetering flight, to be sure, but his mind echoed with the words of *Surfguide* editor Bill Cleary, who had previously traveled to Biarritz and returned with this assessment: "There's good surf and beautiful women—go there."

Stowed below was Fitzpatrick's nine-foot, four-inch, square-tailed surfboard, shaped by his board sponsor, Dave Sweet. Next to it rested a duffel bag stuffed with a dozen clay-wheeled Makaha skateboards, given to

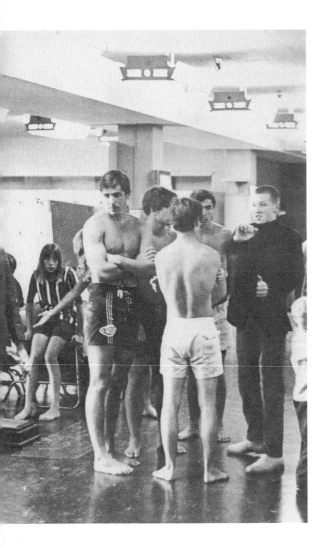

him by Larry Stevenson, *Surfguide* publisher and founder of Makaha Skateboards. Stevenson had told Fitzpatrick, "Here, take these skateboards to Europe and give them away."

The plane took off and the party began. Passengers ordered champagne and brandished flasks, working the flight into a high-altitude lather, the aftermath of which Fitzpatrick recorded in his journal as "a monstrous hangover." Roughly twenty hours and a handful of layovers later, the plane touched down in Paris, where, Fitzpatrick wrote, "mass confusion" set in. Some luggage had been lost, some surfboards damaged. Kraus, who spoke some French, translated what he could of the cussing between irate, lethargic Americans and fed-up, pompous customs agents. Fortunately for Fitzpatrick, his surfboard and duffel bag had arrived with the plane and intact. He whipped out a skateboard and at that moment likely became the first person to ever skateboard in the Paris airport (for whatever it's worth). The airport crowd—amused, intrigued—grew too thick for him to keep at it for more than a few minutes. Same thing would happen later at the base of the Eiffel Tower.

Checked in and set free, Fitzpatrick and his uncle skipped the train to the coast and set out to find their own transportation. Uncle Bob bought a cream-colored VW squareback. After spending a day visiting Paris's requisite tourist traps—the Eiffel Tower, the Arc de Triomph, the Seine—and devouring fine food, beer, and wine, they made for the coast via Chartres and Poitiers. At each stop, Fitzpatrick skateboarded before gathering crowds. "I was mainly just cruising," Fitzpatrick recalls. "I could do handstands, 360s, and nose-wheelies. I'd put on a show if people stopped to watch. I was pretty good at hamming it up, and it wasn't an intimidating setting, it wasn't against the law. People were stunned. And the cool thing about it was that it wasn't just kids that freaked out. Everybody freaked out. They would stand and look in amazement."

One roadside crowd witnessed Fitzpatrick pay for

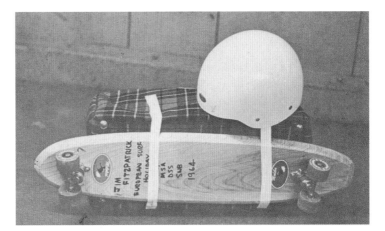

FOREMOST, SURFING WAS OUR MOST SACRED SPORT, BUT WE LOVED SKATEBOARDING EQUAL TO SURFING IN A LOT OF WAYS

DANNY BEARER

national beverage, Fitzpatrick busted out a few skateboards, and he and a handful of newfound friends skated the streets of Biarritz, singing "The Cat Came Back" over and over again as they swerved around town late into the night, searching for smooth concrete. Local kids watched with want and envy.

Following Stevenson's wish, Fitzpatrick gave away four boards during his week in Biarritz. "An incredibly beautiful girl wanted one," he remembers. "So that was an easy giveaway."

Hooked on this new realm—as if an entire village of fifteen- to twenty-year-old California surfers had been beamed to the coast of France—they spent their daylight hours nursing hangovers, eating new foods, drinking wine, making new friends, courting adorable girls, and surfing unforgettable waves. "We were surfing at five or six different places," Fitzpatrick recalls. "St. Jean de Luz was the amazing one because it was this sandy beach peak, and we paddled down to the river and surfed on the border between Spain and France, and there were Spanish guards on the sea wall. This was when Franco still ran the country. And there was this amazing peak, like [Hawaii's] Ala Moana. Perfect rights and lefts peeling in both directions. If

some of that fun as he bombed a smooth hill next to traffic backed up by a passing train. "I heard the terrible noise of the [wheel] bearings slipping in the carrier and watched them spread out across the road in front of me," he recalls. "I got the gnarliest road rash." The next day, Fitzpatrick joined the rest in Biarritz, where the mayor welcomed the surfers, about eighty in all, with a key to the city and a grand banquet flooded with Bordeaux champagne. Absurdly drunk on the you went right, you went into Spain, and if you went left, you went into France. The water was warm and the wind was blowing offshore and it was like a tropical experience. And every time we surfed toward Spain, the guards would lower their submachine guns at us, a gesture of, 'Come too close and we'll blow you apart.' That was really cool."

After a week in Biarritz, during which he placed fourth in a surfing contest against much older competitors, Fitzpatrick stashed his surfboard at Joe Moraiz's surf shop, loaded up his shrinking cache of Makaha skateboards, and took off in the squareback with his uncle and an adult couple for a monthlong lap through thirteen countries. He skateboarded in every city along the way. Hanging nose-wheelies in Spain and Portugal. Carving the French Riviera in Marseilles and the Mediterranean coast down the boot to Naples. Spinning 360s through Switzerland, Austria, Germany, the Netherlands, and across the Channel to England and Ireland. "I would go exploring on my skateboard," he remembers. "It separated me from [my uncle and his friends], and it separated me from everybody else because nobody had ever seen a skateboard before. The impression I got from everybody was that this was something fundamentally different and that they'd never seen it before.

"I would meet kids . . . I'd be skating by myself and somebody would watch me and we'd communicate and I'd let somebody try it and he'd fall down and we'd laugh and I'd give it to him and walk back to the hotel. I came home with one board."

BORN IN SAN DIEGO'S BALBOA HOSPITAL on February 10, 1948, James Edward Fitzpatrick grew up surrounded by watermen. Living in Bird Rock, two blocks from Surf Rock, in a neighborhood he describes as "the ghetto of La Jolla back then," Fitzpatrick was a curious observer of his community's subsistence existence. Families and reclusive bachelors fished for surf perch, calico bass, and halibut. They hunted the tide pools and near-shore boulders, stuffing their game bags with red abalone, spiny lobster, and eel. "My dad and his high school friends would take us down to Mission Bay, to Crystal Pier," Fitzpatrick remembers. "They'd swim around the pier, and to me it looked like they were swimming to the edge of the world. They'd sail, too, in the bay, and body surf with their

> WE'D GO TO BELLAGIO, REVERE. THOSE WERE PLACES THAT THE MAKAHA TEAM ORIGINALLY FOUND, AND WE WERE GOING TO THOSE AND SKATING SURF-STYLE ON THOSE BANKS TEN YEARS BEFORE PERALTA AND THOSE GUYS WERE DOING IT. . . . HEY, BY THE WAY, I WAS A SHITTY SKATEBOARDER; I DIDN'T LIKE IT. I LIKE TO FALL ON WATER. I'M A SURFER. LET'S GET THAT STRAIGHT
> JIM GANZER

RIDING A FREE PUBLIC SKATEBOARD PARK THAT JIM FITZPATRICK VEHEMENTLY
LOBBIED FOR, JAMES O'MAHONEY, FIFTY-EIGHT, CARVE-GRINDS THE TACO-LIP WALL AT
SKATERS POINT, SANTA BARBARA WATERFRONT, SUMMER 2002

PHOTO: SCOTT STARR

arms back. Body surfing was pretty aggressive back then, more valid to these guys than surfing because you're really in the wave."

Young Fitzpatrick took to water naturally, and by the time he was eight or so, he and his buddies were riding their bikes down to Surf Rock to ride inflatable surf mats. "We'd go to the gas station and fill them up rock-solid for more speed. But they leaked a bit and would soften in the cold water, so we'd rest for a while and leave them out in the sun to stiffen up again. We got to our knees eventually, then started to stand up on them, holding on to the rope for stability." Fitzpatrick wouldn't seriously take up surfing until a few years later, but he did get a few tastes of it when older kids let him borrow their boards after he had volunteered to drag the ten-foot lunkers down to the beach.

Then one day, as the classic story goes, the waves were flat and Fitzpatrick and his friends were bored. Hanging out in the driveway of his father's friend Buster Wilson, Fitzpatrick and Buster's sons were getting antsy, looking for something to do. "Here," Buster told them. "Do this." And he showed them how to

build a skateboard by nailing a dismantled roller skate to a short length of lumber. (Buster and Fitzpatrick's father had nailed together similar poor-boy toys during the Depression, topping off the contraptions with T-bar handles or wooden orange crates.) The boys' boredom quickly evaporated on that summer's day in 1957. "We only skated in the summer, and every summer we made our own boards," he remembers. "They would last about an hour. Everything would just rattle free and fall apart. We used one-by-twelves. Nailed the skate down with roofing nails—the broad heads snugged down the roller-skate wheels. It never dawned on me to secure them with a through-hole.

"I'd skate four blocks to my friend's house—a real trek on steel wheels—and we'd go skate down at Bird Rock Elementary School. And we used to like to piss off my grandma. She had made the 'big move' to louvered windows to let in the afternoon breeze, and if they were closed and I skated by, they would rattle and she'd get pissed. That was a fun thing to do, piss off Granny."

In 1960, Fitzpatrick's filmmaker father moved the family to Los Angeles, and for three hundred dollars a month they rented a four-bedroom seaside house built on pilings at the mouth of Malibu's Topanga Canyon. During high tide, the Pacific Ocean swirled under the Fitzpatrick home. Showing up with his homemade skateboard, Fitzpatrick cruised down the gentle concrete slope of the old Pacific Coast Highway as down-canyon breezes pushed plumes of salty mist from the tops of peelers angling off the point. Along the water-

WE'D START AT THE TOP OF LAS FLORES CANYON SO YOU COULD LOOK OVER TO THE SAN FERNANDO VALLEY AND THEN ON THE OTHER SIDE YOU'D BE LOOKING AT THE OCEAN. WE'D TAKE OFF FROM THE TOP THERE AND GET IN A TUCK AND HIT FORTY-FIVE TO FIFTY MILES PER HOUR AND JUST GO AROUND CORNERS AT FORTY MILES PER HOUR AND MAKE IT ALL THE WAY TO THE BOTTOM. YOU DIDN'T GET OUT OF A TUCK. YOU STAYED IN YOUR TUCK AND YOU MADE THE WHOLE RUN CUZ THE MINUTE YOU GOT OUT OF YOUR TUCK, YOU'D GO INTO HIGH-SPEED WOBBLES AND THEN YOU'RE HISTORY. GOODBYE. YOU'D BLOW APART, AND IF YOU BLOW APART AT FORTY MILES PER HOUR, YOU'RE GONE. YOU'RE GOING DOWN. YOU WANNA TALK ABOUT ROAD RASH . . .
WOODY WOODWARD

front and back in the canyon, eccentric writers and off-the-grid artists created and cavorted, savored and subsisted, and grew stinkweed in remote ravines. In the water, territorial surfers carved the consistent right—sometimes called Little Malibu or the Other Malibu—and lashed out at unwelcome visitors. While his father commuted to Hollywood to work forty-eight-hour days, Fitzpatrick took up surfing—scoring

DANNY BEARER, MARQUEZ ELEMENTARY SCHOOL, PACIFIC PALISADES, 1965
PHOTO: JAMES GREGORY

a lousy eight-foot, six-inch foam single-fin for sixty dollars through an ad in the *Evening Outlook*—and soon found his way near the top of the offshore lineup, looked after and tacitly mentored by the old guard, including *Surfguide* editor Bill Cleary—who rented the bottom floor of the Fitzpatrick home—and his friend Mickey Dora, a legendary and often feared surfer mythologized by his own mystique and a background bathed in royalty and wealth.

"I know people who were terrified of Dora," Fitzpatrick remembers. "They thought when he was surfing at Malibu that he was going out of his way to find them and hurt them. That wasn't true. But you didn't want to take off in front of him. He wouldn't seek you out and run you over, but his expectation was that if you were stupid enough to not avoid him, then you deserved to get run over. And I share that same sentiment. He trained me well in that regard.

"And I can remember catching a wave at Topanga in front of Bob Cooper and he was saying, 'Go! Go! Go!' So I dropped in and he surfed right up behind me and he was talking in my ear: 'Come on! Let's go, let's go! C'mon! Trim it up, trim it up! Let's go!' And I was ready to pull out because the section was coming up and I knew I wasn't going to make it and he was yelling, 'Don't pull out! Let's go! Let's go!' And he literally coached me through this wave and we got all the way down and he said, 'I thought you were going to chicken-shit out of there.' And I said, 'Yeah, I did too.' And he said, 'Well, yeah, you made it.' My surfing, at that moment, went from an apprehensive level to a light-year ahead. It was a phenomenal experience."

As Fitzpatrick and his young friends—namely the Saenz brothers, Paul Molloy, Mike Malloy, Bob Elliot, and Woody Woodward, among others—eased through their teens, they naturally assumed control of who was allowed to surf their wave. They donned army surplus jackets and called themselves the Topanga Beach Bombers. "We were an anti-club," Fitzpatrick explains. "Essentially a gang. We got in fights, stole cars, and pissed off our parents. We would be at a party and the night would come down to a girl or some alcohol and there'd be a big fight. If people snuck onto our beach, we'd knock them out and break into their cars. I can still remember the first time I found a bag of pot in somebody's car."

Woodward, whose parents' paddle-tennis court was a favorite Topanga skate spot, adds, "All the beaches were very clannish. You were entering someone else's water, and you were either accepted or not. It's like every beach had a gang. And it still goes on to this day."

As Cleary's upstairs neighbor and fellow Topanga surfer, Fitzpatrick often hitched rides to *Surfguide's* Santa Monica headquarters, where Larry Stevenson was always busy with his magazine. Stevenson, who had grown up in a state orphanage in the '30s, held vivid memories of a visit by actor Leo Carrillo, who had given the boys skate scooters for Christmas. More than two decades later, Stevenson sensed that skateboards could ride the coattails of surfing's surge in popularity, and, in 1963, he founded Makaha Skateboards, running ads in his magazine featuring famous surfers, such as Mike Hynson and Mike Doyle, giving props to Stevenson's clay-wheeled sidewalk surfboards. Surf legend Phil Edwards, too, was integral

BEFORE THE SKATEBOARD-TEAM DAYS, WE WERE DOING THE [SWIMMING] POOLS ON THE CHICAGO ROLLER WHEELS, AND THAT WAS HAIRBALL, MAN, CUZ YOU COULD JUST SPIN OUT. I MEAN, YOU'D SEE HOW FAR YOU COULD PUSH IT, BUT IT WAS UNREAL CUZ YOU COULD GET VERTICAL ON THE WALL. AND THAT WAS BACK THEN. AND THEN THESE GUYS GOT THE NEW [URETHANE] WHEELS TEN YEARS LATER AND TOOK IT TO A NEW DIMENSION
GEORGE TRAFTON

to Makaha's development and success, his soul-arched silhouette gracing his own signature model.

Fitzpatrick, a surfer foremost but clearly an experienced skateboarder, was in the right place at the right time. "Cleary gave me my first clay-wheeled skateboard," he remembers. "I had one of the first five prototypes. And I think maybe for a day or a month or maybe a few months, I was the Makaha skateboard team. I mean, the concept of a team . . . there wasn't really any reason to have a team." But by summer 1964, he estimates, a bonafide team (one of skateboarding's earliest) would take shape, lavished with free skateboards and matching nylon jackets of navy blue and chrome. Levis and single-pocket tees completed the outfit, along with a pair of Topsiders or Jack Purcells with the big nub toe. A Pendleton if it was chilly.

Over the next few years, countless teams would form as skateboarding swelled to its first peak of popularity before dying down practically overnight in late 1965, fizzling when it began to be plagued by widespread injuries. Fitzpatrick, too, would eventually fade from the scene as he started going out with girls (especially after scoring his first ride, a 1961 VW Microbus) and helping his father to produce films (he took over the business entirely in 1968 after his father died suddenly of a massive heart attack), and as his own abilities were eclipsed by Makaha's more dedicated skateboarders.

Before the wave crashed, however, Stevenson became a very rich man, reportedly selling four million dollars in boards within three years. *Surfguide* editor Cleary and assistant art director Jim Ganzer—who would launch Jimmy'Z clothing in 1984—coaxed the stoke by passing out free boards to kids around town and recruiting a crew of the area's best riders, young innovators who put down the first roots of sidewalk surfing's stylistic aesthetic. Ganzer's recollection: "George Trafton, Danny Bearer, and Torger Johnson were the main guys, and John Freis, and Woody [Woodward] in the juniors division."

As the team's first Captain Makaha, surfer Dave "Mr. Head Dip" Rochlen (who rode for his hero, Dewey Weber) drove the kids around to small demonstrations, but mainly to practice their turns on asphalt banks in neighborhood schoolyards. Not too long into his gig, however, Rochlen was lured from Makaha as the skate-board branch of Hobie Surfboards caught the building momentum of skateboarding's first wave. Hobie launched a partnership with Vita Pakt Orange Juice, owned and backed by the power and fame and wealth of the Hilton hotel family. The young Hilton brothers, Dave (who in 1964 appeared on the first cover of *Skateboard Quarterly*) and Steve, were both up-and-coming surfers and first-generation skateboarders.

Rochlen recalls: "Baron Hilton knew my family from my uncle [the now deceased David Gayle Rochlen, Sr.], the famous Santa Monica Beach lifeguard who was on the cover of *Life* magazine. He was really good friends with [Hilton] down in Sorrento, where they had their big ocean house, and taught him how to surf and stuff. Anyway, Hobie seduced me away [from Makaha] . . . and some of the kids made the switchover, too. You know, riding for Hobie was a lot more impressive to a young kid."

"It made me feel bad" when the kids left Makaha for Hobie, remembers Stevenson, now battling Parkinson's at a rest home in Ventura, California. "But they [the Hiltons] had all the tools. They had the hotels. They could offer the whole group a free trip to Hawaii, and I had to borrow money to keep up with them."

Fitzpatrick, too, was lured to the Hobie name, but only in the water. He switched over from the Dave Sweet team after he returned from the European Surfing Holiday and Rochlen opened a Hobie surf shop in Santa Monica. Fitzpatrick and Rochlen had also surfed together with the Santa Monica Surfing Association. On the asphalt, Fitzpatrick stuck with Makaha as *Surfguide* columnist Bob Feigel took over for a spell as team manager, later replaced by Ganzer, who recruited new riders and hauled them around at first in his 1950 Ford Woody, then in a more dependable 1956 bronze-and-white Chevy Nomad. These mini–skate safaris took the boys along the fresh ribbons

of asphalt streaming from Sunset Mesa to the peak of Las Flores Canyon Road for forty-mile-an-hour speed runs back down, and around town to Beverly Hills parking garages and the overhead asphalt banks swelling from neighborhood schoolyards, the same slopes where Dogtown's Z-Boys would carve history with urethane wheels a decade later.

"Going to Paul Revere [Junior High], going to Brentwood [Elementary], going to Bellagio [Elementary] was phenomenal," Fitzpatrick remembers. "Going to Bellagio was like going to Waimia Bay or Sunset Beach—it was about getting to the bottom without dying. The skate trips had the same gestalt as the surf trips, like the European Surfing Holiday. You'd go to this place to go surfing, and maybe there's a crowd, maybe there's waves, maybe it's windy. And you'd go to this skate spot—I mean, I remember going to Bellagio and it seemed like another part of the world. Just big and glassy and no one out."

FOUR DECADES LATER, FITZPATRICK is the principal of Santa Barbara's Montessori School, which he, along with his wife and two other teachers, founded in 1975. His close-cut brown hair shows only traces of gray. He's tanned and fit, his youthful blue eyes knocking ten years from his fifty-five.

When he's not running the school, spending time with his family, or surfing world-class Rincon, Fitzpatrick acts as executive director of the International Association of Skateboard Companies (IASC), a trade group composed of most of the industry's movers and shakers. Fitzpatrick helped to launch the IASC in 1994, a year after leaving a six-year run orchestrating various promotions for Powell Skateboards, one of the largest and oldest skateboard companies.

"In '91, '92, skateboarding was starting to shrivel up," he says. "Right before I left Powell, I sent a fax to all the companies, saying, essentially, 'I've been on the board of SIMA [the Surf Industry Manufacturers

I SURFED THAT RIGHT POINT [AT TOPANGA] EVERY DAY, AND SOMETIMES I WAS OUT THERE THINKING TO MYSELF, "I WISH SOMEBODY WOULD COME OUT AND SURF WITH ME."

JIM FITZPATRICK

Association] for the last two years, and SIMA was doing stuff outside of the business world that was helping surfing, and I was thinking we should do this too, [and promoting] skateparks would be a good way.' I sent out this fax, and nothing happened."

But about a year later, Fitzpatrick got a call from a few industry heads keen on starting an association, and within a few meetings a board of directors was elected, with Fitzpatrick at its helm. They put together a mission statement that originally decreed that its primary goal was to "promote the business of skateboarding." Then it was suggested that this be shortened to "promote skateboarding," a change Fitzpatrick considers a philosophical step in the right direction, one that, at least in part, removes money from the equation.

"Within the first eighteen months [of the IASC's formation]," he says, "I got a call from Kevin Thatcher [former editor of *Thrasher* magazine], who told me to call state assemblyman Bill Morrow. Apparently somebody on the House floor had held up a *Thrasher* with a full-page picture of a skateboarder sliding down a handrail along some sidewalk somewhere, and [the politician] was saying, 'This has got to stop.' But on the facing page, there was a Fuct clothing ad showing nude chicks with stickers on their nipples or something, and that's what really captured the attention of a lot of lawmakers. Anyway, his point was that kids were 'endangering lives' and that there was too much conflict between skateboarders and pedestrians. And Morrow became interested in changing the liability laws so that we could get skateparks built easier."

Backed by the IASC's top agenda item—"promote skateboarding"—Fitzpatrick launched an unprecedented push to cool California's notoriously sue-happy personality and to knock down tall walls between skateboarders and paths to public skateboard parks. "It was just as difficult to educate the skateboard industry as it was to educate the politicians," he says. "A lot of companies were like, 'Who cares? We don't need parks.' And my point was always: If there's a park, then the kids will always have a place to skate, so there will always be a need for equipment, and with families getting involved, the sport will grow."

Between 1995 and 1997, through Web sites and magazine ads, the IASC received postcards, letters, and petitions—seventy-five thousand pieces of mail in all. Fitzpatrick stuffed tens of thousands of letters into a sack, bought himself a sportcoat on the IASC's tab, and drove to Sacramento. "It was classic *Mr. Smith Goes to Washington*," he remembers. "I mean, it's kind of corny, but it really was a grassroots political statement. [The politicians] asked me why we should do this, and I said, 'Because all these kids want it to happen.' I ended up pointing fingers at legislators, because they didn't want the law changed because they were protecting the rights of skateboarders to sue if they got injured. Essentially, I said, 'Fuck you, we don't want that sort of protection. We want to be able to skateboard—if we get hurt, it's our own fault.'"

In 1998, California lawmakers put skateboarding on the state's "hazardous recreational activities" list, thereby making it more difficult for a skateboarder to sue a city if he or she gets hurt on public property. When Fitzpatrick launched his drive in 1995, scarcely a handful of public skateparks existed in California.

Now that number approaches two hundred.

CLEARLY, FITZPATRICK'S ONE of a handful of first-generation skateboarders who have really given something back—to this dull-day activity that sat him down in his friend's driveway to build steel-wheeled boards from scratch; to this crowd-pleasing sidewalk surf that sent him across Europe to give away clay-wheeled boards; to this subculture business that supported his family though the late-'80s surge; to this way of life that convinced him that every town should have a public skatepark because, after all, no matter how many laws are passed to banish them, skateboarders are always going to skateboard.

Fitzpatrick's own ride was a forty-four-and-a-half-inch-long Powell skateboard, a gift from his fellow workers when he quit the company in 1993. For years it stood against the wall near the door of Fitzpatrick's office, where he'd grab it daily for a quick carve across the playground, looking less like a modern-day school principal than a surfer with deep roots in the '60s. Sporting Independent trucks and soft wheels for easy cruising, the longboard's underside, appropriately, was silkscreened with a silhouette of Fitzpatrick as a young man nose-riding a sweet wave crumbling off Topanga Beach—the board and its image a blend of two ocean-born worlds, a gold watch for his longevity, and a smooth ride down memory lane.

Until some kid ripped it off.

3

POOLS

MILKBONE
SUMMER

ONE OF THE GREATEST SUMMERS OF ADAM "CHILI" STERN'S LIFE ACTUALLY BEGAN IN EARLY SPRING. LIKE MOST SERIOUS POOL SKATERS, HE HAD NOTICED THAT THE WINTER OF 2001–2002 WAS MARKED BY DROUGHT THROUGHOUT SOUTHERN CALIFORNIA AND THAT ABUNDANT SPRING

SHOWERS, TOO, HAD FAILED TO COME.

SHOWERS, TOO, HAD FAILED TO COME. Chili and his closest friends, the handful of men he regularly rode with, were fired up: pool-skating season started early that year.

BY SAINT PATRICK'S DAY, Chili and crew had stretched their legs out at a few of their standbys from the previous season, such as the hilltop View Pool overlooking Malibu Point and a fast, kidney-bean-shaped bowl on the outskirts of Burbank. Around April Fool's Day, with the weather providing much more sun than rain, they took advantage of the dry spell to clean out and skate another handful of pools—some fun ones, certainly, but nothing to dream about—before triple-digit summer temperatures cut short their sessions. As daylight savings time added an hour to their early-evening pool hunts, Chili sniffed out a few virgin bowls, the best of which, the dreamy Hallmark Pool, on a completely subjective scale from one to 99—there's no such thing as a perfect pool, thus no grade of 100—ranked well into the 90s, a solid A. These gems, as they're called, are few and far between. And to locate, clean, and session a gem steadily before Cinco de Mayo was indeed a great start to a promising summer of pool skating.

To a pool skater, a great and lengthy season of backyard bowl riding ranks extremely high on his or her favorite-things-in-life list, up there with good grub, drinking with friends, live rock and roll, hot sex, and sound sleep. It's an obsession and a lust and a life filled with extensive exploration, addictive mystery, high risk, giddy anticipation, back-breaking labor, and, ultimately, unforgettable secret sessions shared among the best of friends.

By summer's end that memorable year, Chili and company had bagged dozens of bowls, and much of

the hard luck and hard work of pool skating—the dead-end searches, the mucky clean-outs, the fits of depression brought on by the loss of a gem—had passed. They had enough good, round bowls lined up to spend hours on their boards, rather than burning daylight on the hunt or on cleaning out some mediocre rectangular pool.

ONE OF THOSE DAYS PLAYED out like a pool skater's cream dream—a long afternoon of roomy round bowls and a van full of friends, topped off with dive-bar booze. And it also served as a fitting farewell, an Indian-summer nightcap after an extended season of pool skating throughout the arid expanse of greater Southern California. Chili had recently accepted a job offer on Hawaii's Big Island, and this day would be his last backyard bowl mission on the mainland for almost a year.

All but one of the skaters in Chili's '92 Ford Aerostar minivan called Santa Barbara home. Chili was at the wheel. He was thirty-five, six foot three, lanky and flexible, born and raised in San Jose, where he started skating at the age of ten and bought his first board—flat, skinny, made of fiberglass—for eight bucks from the older kid down the block. First skated Winchester park in 1978. Once witnessed legendary Steve Caballero rip Campbell skatepark a new one. Took a break from skating in college to chase well-hit golf balls, a talent that took him and the rest of the Cal State San Bernardino golf team to a division-three fourth place nationally. Occasionally, he'd drive out to Palm Springs to sneak onto high-end golf courses.

Sitting shotgun, in the navigator's post, was Scott "SP" Power, thirty-five, barefoot, handsome in that square-bodied, tanned-and-blue-eyed, '60s surfer kind of way. Working part-time installing fins on freshly built surfboards, SP typically dragged himself from bed at daybreak, pulled down a great wage by midmorning, and spent the rest of his day surfing, skating, browsing thrift stores, or all of the above. His uncluttered,

HERBIE FLETCHER CARVING "THE POOL,"
STANTON, CALIFORNIA, CIRCA 1963
PHOTO COURTESY OF HERBIE FLETCHER

I MOSTLY LIKE JUST SKATING WITH MY FRIENDS AND HANGING OUT WITH THEM, AND WE'RE KINDA OLD, AND POOL SKATING IS AN OLD STYLE, AND YOU DON'T HAVE TO BE A SUPERSTAR TO ENJOY IT. PLUS, FINDING POOLS IS HALF THE FUN

ADAM "CHILI" STERN

purist lifestyle shone through in his simple yet stylish wave riding and pool skating and his disdain of shoes. Each year he toasted his late-April birthday by partying with friends and skating the infamous and now-buried Nude Bowl, a gem of a kidney on the high-desert fringes of Palm Springs.

Piled in the back of the van was Byron Ramey, thirty, down from San Francisco for a weekend of pool skating and Chili's big send-off, and SP's housemate Tony Capalby, thirty, who made rent by applying the final

touches to top-of-the-line surfboards. Mike Kresky, who, six months prior, had celebrated his fortieth birthday at a somewhat secret Central Coast surf shanty with a homemade pool tucked away in the backyard, sat on the floor of the van, studying Ernest Sheldon Booth's *Mammals of Southern California*.

During the drive down to Los Angeles, they passed flat seas at surfing's famous Rincon right and porpoises riding waist-high waves at La Conchita.

They knew their first pool of the day, around 11 A.M., would be a quick hit, just something to shake out their road legs and kick-start the blood. She was an eight-foot-deep, baby-blue, egg-shaped bowl built by Blue Haven Pools in the middle of a fully occupied apartment complex near a major crossroads somewhere between Santa Barbara and Los Angeles. Since they'd been promptly kicked out of this one before, their game plan was simple: frenzy to get in as many runs as possible before they were given the boot.

Within five minutes of the first rebounding echoes of hard urethane wheels buzzing across ceramic tiles, the landlady erupted from her corner unit, beelining straight for Tony, whom she must have recognized from the last time he barged this pool. She wasn't happy. "I don't understand why you do this here," she shot in her heavy Mexican accent. Before she had even finished her sentence, Tony was heading back to the van without a word. Chili and Byron tried to sweet-talk her, probably offering her a few dollars for a fifteen-minute session. But their bad breath fell on deaf ears.

By high noon, Chili had slowly laced through the lunch-hour traffic hell blanketing most of Los Angeles, parking two blocks from a long-abandoned hotel. Not so long ago, skaters could park front and center in the hotel's side lot before hopping an ineffectual security gate. That was before the grumpy next-door neighbor witnessed such trespassing. From that moment on, he was known as "the hater next door," the surrogate security guard who'd mean-mug any passersby while jotting down their license-plate numbers. After being sent away once by the nasty old raisin, Chili and crew soon figured out that a few-minute sidewalk ride around the front of the faded building could put them at the gate without being spotted. And once inside, surrounded by the towering ski-lodge-esque courtyard walls, they were completely out of eye- and earshot of an outside world bustling with paranoid neighbors and prowling patrol cars.

But as they stealthily approached the entrance on this day, spirits dropped. From the top of the black gate rose a barrier banged together from two-by-fours, cyclone fencing, and barbed wire, slanting back a good six feet and nailed into place along the tall, adjacent walls. The over-the-top gate hop, the only known porthole to the bone-dry bowl within, had been sealed off. Reactions: "Fuck." "Shit." "This, after that fucking hell drive."

"Hold on," Tony said, climbing halfway up the wrought-iron gate. He tugged on the bottom corner of the new barrier. It budged. Scrambling carefully past rusty spikes, Tony eased his way over the barbed barricade

and onto the slanted roof, where he could put some weight behind a well-placed kung-fu kick. He bashed until it hinged free. Below, Chili excitedly scanned behind a nearby dumpster for something with which to wedge open the loosened barrier.

"Watch it!" Kresky warned Chili. But it was too late. "Awww, you just stepped in some human gang-gang."

"Fuck," Chili said, supremely grossed out, scanning for a patch of grass, some dead leaves, a discarded shirt, anything on which to wipe his crap-caked shoe.

"Yeah, last time I was here, there was a bum sacked out right there," Tony said, pointing to the narrow piss-stench passage between the dumpster and the hotel wall. "And it was a she-bum."

"There's nothing worse than stepping in bum shit," Byron added matter-of-factly. Then SP, with a desiccated sarcasm so goddamned understated it sounded sincere: "I heart stepping in bum chads."

Kresky swiftly assumed the search, found an eight-foot rusted pole, and, as Tony powered the barrier free and lifted its edge, quickly propped the whole shebang wide open. They handed over their pad bags and a push broom, then scampered over undetected and power walked toward the center courtyard through semi enclosed halls haunted by neo-Nordic architecture, fragmented flagstones, waist-high copper ash-trays, and dusty ice dispensers. And there she was.

The pool was a nine-foot-deep bowl bent to the left, but because it sported a bonus pocket in the shallow end, which threw its shape out of tradition, it couldn't be called a true kidney. Like most hotel pools, this one was built to refresh a gaggle of vacationers; hence, she was bigger than an average backyard bowl, with a wide shallow end for the waders and a roomy deep end for diving. Topping forest-green tiles, her coping was composed of large-aggregate polished pebbles that sent out loud, echoing barks with even the most exploratory of frontside scrapes. Her only flaws were a slight kink running halfway through the deep end and a yardlong, slightly overhanging bulge protruding from

I'D RATHER GET THAN CHECK OUT

CLOCKWISE, FROM LEFT:
BRETT TURNER THROWS TWO OUT OF A STEEP, TIGHT BOWL IN
JACKSONVILLE, FLORIDA, FEBRUARY 2003
PHOTO: RHINO
MARTY GRIMES, ROCKINGHAM POOL,
WEST LOS ANGELES, CALIFORNIA, 1978
PHOTO: © GLEN E. FRIEDMAN
AARON MILES GODOY FRONTSIDE-GRINDS FROM DEEP TO
SHALLOW AT BUENA VISTA, SANTA CRUZ COUNTY, CIRCA 1990
PHOTO: CHRIS KARDAS

TONY ALVA, DOG BOWL, SANTA MONICA, CALIFORNIA, 1977
PHOTO: © GLEN E. FRIEDMAN
PAT SMITH, NEW JERSEY, AUGUST 2002
PHOTO: RHINO

SHOT IN THE HEAD THE WARPED TOUR

TONY CAPALBY

the right side wall. SP hopped in and started sweeping a light scatter of leaves and deep-end debris into a dustpan, then pulled on some socks and a pair of black high-top Converse Chuck Taylor All Stars.

"Man, she looks good," Kresky said, to himself mostly, already lost in lines he'd been mentally tracing from the moment he had first laid eyes on her. As he sat on the shallow-end steps, strapping on his well-worn Rector knee pads, his eyes drew long, smoothly arching paths from the shallow end up to the tiles, over the light on the deep-end face wall, back low along the side wall, and straight for a shallow-end pocket that, if he could follow these mental sketchings while standing on his skateboard, would pull him in and spit him out again, speeding toward the deep. In a skateboarder's world, lines are everywhere. On the streets, for example, a nervous-system matrix of routes connects a skater's front door to the liquor store two blocks away. On the road, Chili's drive through the concrete jungle was an efficient weave deeply influenced by his skateboard-bred knack for looking far down a path and improvising as new channels open up. In a pool, finding lines is the key to milking speed from concrete curves that bend and stretch vertically, horizontally, diagonally, and at all angles.

"Yeah," Chili chimed in, sitting on the shallow-end steps, pulling a Pro Design pad over his right elbow and tightening up the laces on his Emericas. "Side-wall tumor is kinda lame, but that bonus pocket is baaaaaaaaad" (as in not at all bad, as in good, as in great, as in exceptionally kick-ass).

A few minutes into the session, Kresky was already sweating, a red bandanna hoisting his strawberry-blond dreadlocks out of his face. "I just wanna get a fuckin' grind."

"The man's hungry," SP noticed, sweat darkening the edges of his salty ballcap.

Then Tony: "You gotta want it."

Clearly, Byron wanted it, and he stayed on through a frontside grind over the face-wall light and a few coping blocks beyond, barely staying on through the buckling kink below.

"Whoa!" came the chorus from the shallow end, where the rest waited. "Nice one."

Half an hour into the session, and everybody's lines were looking smoother and faster. SP was milking his highly polished figure-8 line, taking it easy on his knee, still recovering from a painful hyperextension weeks back in San Diego's Pala Round Pool. Kresky was cutting some loud backside carve grinds through the deep and tapping some untouched trannies on the hip. Before long, Tony was on deck, looking at a roll-in line. After a few tester approach runs, he pushed once along the pitted flagstone deck, heading at a slight angle for the top edge of the deep-end pocket. With just enough speed at the edge, he committed, tipping his upper body into the pool. His lower body and board instantly followed, and he went from standing on his board on the pool deck to riding straight down the deep-end wall. But the free fall from the coping to the lower reaches of vertical proved too disorienting, and he slipped from his board, plowing his lead shoulder and TSG elbow pad into the opposite wall. It was a tough slam, but Tony got up laughing and, under his breath, said, "I got that, I got that." He practically jogged back to his spot, where he pushed off without hesitation. And made it. Cleanly.

"Whoa!" came the shallow-end chorus. "Yeah, Tony."

Tony took a seat on the middle step, his smile revealing the thin gap between his front teeth, looking a lot like a slimmed-down Jack Black. "That was such a long drop," he panted. "It was gnarly. Scared me." Now that he was really warmed up, he set his sights on "the enchilada."

Every pool has a few obstacles to negotiate, the eas-

YOU REALLY DO HAVE TO HAVE FUN WITH IT. YOU CAN'T INVEST YOUR EGO TOO MUCH. DON'T TAKE YOURSELF TOO SERIOUSLY. AND THE LATEST STUFF, THE BOARD, THE GRAPHICS, THE HOTTEST SHOE, ALL THAT SHIT IS ANTITHETICAL TO THE TRUE SPIRIT OF SKATEBOARDING. IT'S ABOUT YOUR SHITTY PAIR OF VANS AND YOUR SKATE AND JUST GOIN' WITH IT. GETTIN' SOME

MIKE KRESKY

iest of which is the light, usually located dead center on the deep-end face wall. "Going over the light" is the most basic benchmark for a pool skater, something beginners strive for, something veterans don't even have to think about (unless the pool is the most challenging of abysmal pits). Elsewhere on the face wall usually gapes the deathbox, the considerable void through which, in a full pool, water drains to the pump and filter. Deathboxes are always located just under the coping, where the waterline would be in a full pool, and are roughly as wide as a coping block and as tall as a tile. Typically they loom just out of reach of most face-wall grinds, often tucked away in some tight pocket or along some mid-shallow flat wall—that is, they're usually a challenge to grind over and thus they're always in a pool skater's crosshairs. As sessions heat up, attempts to grind over the deathbox become more frequent, as do the mumbling taunts. "Get the death yet?" "The deathbox is calling your name." "You got the line to the death, so smash it!" With this crew, going over the light and the deathbox with one drawn-out, high-speed grind was long ago dubbed "the enchilada." It's not just going over the light. It's not just smashing the deathbox. It's the whole enchilada.

And Tony, nearly salivating, dug in admirably for about a dozen attempts. But at this pool, the enchilada seemed out of reach. When Tony found the shallow-end sweet spot and pumped with every ounce of horsepower contained in his stout and stocky frame, carried by tall, rock-hard wheels spinning on ceramic bearings, he was flat-out hauling ass. And he'd carve over the light before locking into the loudest, longest frontside grinds of the day, explosions of abuse against polished rock. But every time, he pulled the rip cord just as his back wheels locked into the box and safely

ran out his bail as the others cooled down poolside, making motions to move on. He had to wait for another day to get this enchilada.

Kresky turned to Chili and asked, "Where's the next hussy?"

AFTER A QUICK EXIT and reinstallation of the dislodged gate-top barbed-wire barrier, they piled back into Chili's van and headed out. Copilot SP, barefoot again, scanned The List, a partially typed, partially hand-scribbled record of the addresses of all known area pools. This late in the season, The List offered a

decent number of "permission pools" (as in, the owners are incredibly cool and allow skaters to ride) but was dominated mostly by "barges" (as in, hop the backyard fence, ride aggressively and quietly, and split before the owners, neighbors, and/or cops catch on). A few pools on The List still needed to be drained, and a few were "door jobs" (as in, the owners required some serious sweet-talking and/or bribing). Occasionally, a door job becomes a permission, but more often the pool's owner is against letting a handful of complete strangers risk serious injury on private property, and, once permission is denied, said door job becomes a barge.

With coordinates from SP, Chili took a few turns off the 405 to a semi-upscale neighborhood a few beats north of the heart of Dogtown, the breeding ground of the infamous Zephyr team's '70s skateboard prodigies, profiled in the 2002 documentary *Dogtown and Z-Boys*.

The high sun was warming the smoggy blue. A cool breeze rose off the ocean, funneling into the van as the young, attractive mothers and cute college students with the best bodies money could buy walked to or from their midday coffee on the corner. With loud-laughing self-mockery, the sweaty vanload gawked like undersexed construction workers. Every woman with any semblance of physical beauty got a hoot or a "Helllllllooooooooo!"

The petite, raven-haired young woman on a corner pay phone got a "Hi there" from Chili, leaning out his window. She turned around and faced the van. Nice chassis, for sure, but she had a beat-up grille.

"Easy, guy," Tony called from the back seat. "She looks like Juan Epstein."

"Who?"

"Juan Epstein, the Puerto Rican Jew from *Welcome Back, Kotter*."

"Puerto Rican Jew?"

"Yeah. Juan Epstein's a Puerto Rican Jew. It's a known fact."

"Puerto Jew?"

"Yeah."

Deeper into the neighborhood, Chili turned into an alley and announced, "Okay, this is a quickie," parking alongside a tall, battered fence with peeling paint, the backyard boundary of an old, empty single-story cottage facing imminent demolition. Within half a minute all of them were over the fence with their boards, plus the broom and dustpan, which, it turned out, weren't needed. Obviously, another crew had skated her recently. In faint black marker on a shallow-end step, a small scrawl urged all skaters to respect the pool. The message was meant well, of course, and was clearly posted by some skater who didn't want this Blue Haven barge overexploited by careless lurkers who leave empty beer cans and vandalize houses. But to many pool skaters, tagging a bowl in any fashion, no matter how miniscule, is sacrilege. Leaving only traces of aluminum and slivers of maple across her perfect lip, Chili and company rode for just fifteen minutes before hopping back into the alley and driving away undetected.

One block north in the same alley, Chili pulled in close to an eight-foot-tall cyclone fence sealing off the backyard of yet another home slated for demolition. Directly across the narrow alley, a pair of carpet-layers were buttoning up their rig. While the rest of the van sat in silence, fingers crossed, Chili rolled down his window and broke the ice with the elder of the two.

"You guys been working here for a while?"

"Just today."

"Um . . . cuz . . . we're going to ride our skateboards in a pool on the other side of that fence there and want to know if you're cool with that."

POOLS ARE THE BEST CUZ THEY'RE NOT MADE TO SKATE. EVERY WALL'S A DIFFERENT CHALLENGE. AND BARGING BACKYARDS, TRESPASSING— IT'S A RUSH

DAVE "SHAGGY" PALMER,
POOL SKATER, SKATEPARK BUILDER

The carpet guy smiled, shrugged, and held up his hands. "Hey, do what you gotta do. It's not my business."

"Cool, thanks," Chili signed off.

Once in the pool—the Screamer, as it was called, after the portrait of a terrified woman that overlooked the deep end from the back wall of the garage—the crew was cupped away, invisible to all neighbors, but, instinctively, they kept their voices low and their heads hunched down slightly. The skateboarding itself was loud, to be sure—all that rock-hard urethane humming across plaster and rattling over tiles, all that aluminum and wood grinding and barking and smacking against concrete coping, all of it echoing around and beyond a big empty hole with good acoustics—but it's better not to lace the music with hoots and above-ground visuals of sweating, bleeding skaters.

As in many other forms of skateboarding, breaking the law is a given in pool skating. Blatant trespassing is the modus operandi, and secretive pool skaters must stay off the radar, not only to protect their scene from kooks who squeal away new pools to all their friends, but also to keep a clean police record. Running from cops has always been part of the deal as well, but with this crew, it's a rarity. If the cops do show up at a pool they're barging, it's far more likely that this crew will simply say hello, cooperate if asked for identification, and, if asked, tell the cops that they heard about the pool from some neighborhood kids who had been riding it for a while. And most of the time, the cops will put away their ticket pads and simply tell them to leave and not come back. Sometimes a curious cop— or one with a son who'd rather ride a skateboard than join the baseball team—will call for a quick show, saying, "Before I kick you guys outta here, I wanna see what you got."

In truth, cops aren't likely to scan neighborhoods for hidden trespassers, and because of that fact, this crew never keeps an eye out for black-and-whites. It's the neighbors they're anxious about. Empty house with an empty pool, perfect—but what if some homebody grandma who hates everything lives next door? She'll call the cops. Guaranteed. So a pool skater must barge, stealthily slipping over the back-alley fence, always keeping one eye on the clock, giving her five minutes to notice that somebody is skating the pool next door, five minutes to call the cops, and five minutes for the cops to show up. In and out in less than fifteen minutes will usually leave a pool skater with a good sweat, some good grinds, and a clean police record.

Back in the Screamer, the fifteen-minute rule wasn't in effect, but they had no mind to push their luck by riding for more than a half hour or so. They'd never been booted from this bowl before—not by some stroke of luck, but precisely because they had always minded that tenuous balance between sharing it with

a handful of friends and keeping it under wraps and limiting sessions to less than thirty minutes.

Kresky had long been part of that handful of trusted friends, that short list of skaters who could count on Chili, SP, and Tony for a good day of bowl riding. Not only could he be trusted with a secret, he was fun to ride with and a pleasure to watch, his loose, definitively old-school style born from New Jersey's Cherry Hill skatepark and Florida's surf scene.

Moving to Santa Barbara in 1985 to earn his teaching credential from UCSB, Kresky found himself drawn to the region's remote backcounty, and by the early '90s was trekking through it on extensive backpacking trips. In raw nature, Kresky found portholes through which he could transcend the hollow-shell personality of the modern Western world, and his study hall shifted from classroom to wilderness, where lessons are inspiring and demanding, humbling and crucial. He conjured fire from sticks and stones, tracked large game across icy rivers, bushwhacked through tick-ridden chaparral, and spent cold nights alone on remote forest floors. During these sojourns, Kresky reconnected to forces made obsolete by humankind's head-down, roughshod race over and away from nature. By 2000, he was also passing along what he had learned: He was selected by inner-city school districts to teach animal tracking and natural history to hard-ass teens with adult police records. Opening fascinating new realms for these kids filled Kresky with pride and a contagious self-confidence, which in part explains how, at forty, when for most the light has long since dimmed, Kresky's skateboarding talents were *improving*.

At the Screamer, however, his talents weren't on point. Almost off the bat, he'd rolled directly over a drain divot in the bottom of the deep end, sending him over the bars and heavily onto his left shoulder. On his next run, he slammed in the same fashion, then took a couple of back-to-back shallow-end slams, folding, at last, like a cheap lawn chair at the bottom of the steps. Whipping plaster dust and blood from his scraped shoulder, he looked at the others gathered on the steps and said, "Just make mine a shit sandwich, please, cuz I'm taking big ol' bites right now." Right then, Byron pushed in and took a nice hipper himself. (Hipper: a contusion of the hip caused by falling on it at high speed.) Byron turned to Kresky and said, "Save half that shit sandwich for me." Kresky laughed, almost a little too loudly, and asked, "Do you want fries with that?"

Slowly, over his years of study, Kresky's concept of the pool-skater way of life had drawn upon what he had learned from nature. The links became clear. Indeed: what pool skaters do is a form of urban tracking. They look for what a tracker would call certain search images—palm trees towering from a backyard, the tops of pool slides jutting over backyard fences, cyclone fences and oversized dumpsters outside a home under remodel. All these signs and more can pull a hunting pool skater toward his or her "prey." There are larger images as well—beat-up neighborhoods in once well-off areas, laced with long alleys stretching like ancient hunting trails between miles of backyards. And, with experience, which comes only with time on the prowl, these search images synthesize and imbue the subconscious with such sensitivity that a veteran pool skater will know intuitively that a certain part of town, even a certain backyard, holds a pool, because *it just feels like there's a pool nearby*.

Kresky's contemplation: "Hunting for pools is a deep, inner drive acted out in a modern context. It's the mythical and heroic search for the Holy Grail. And it's nature acting out through what's available in the modern world, nature playing out its urges. And thank God there are pool skaters, because they are more connected to the primal world than most people."

Sooner rather than later, Chili's instincts were telling him to get the crew out of the Screamer's backyard and move on while there was still plenty of light. Outside the fence, as they loaded back into the Aerostar, a man leaned out a second-story window across the alley.

"Hey, you skateboarders, get out of here!" he yelled, shooing them with one hand. "You, in the black hat, I've got your license-plate number. I'll call the cops. I know your mother's name."

I know your mother's name?—that one set the whole vanload laughing as Chili peeled out. Banking back onto the 405 freeway, Chili was instantly slowed by the greatest given of Los Angeles: traffic. "Aw," he grumbled under his breath. "This is cute" (as in not at all attractive, as in ugly, as in frustratingly disappointing, as in completely fucking lame). Some tunes would help pass the time. From a selection that included Radio Birdman, the Saints, and an AC/DC mixed tape that, naturally, contained only Bon Scott–era songs, Chili popped in the Clash's *London Calling* and eased into the fast lane toward their last pool of the day.

After a falafel stop and a liquor store run for a case of beer, they did a slow-roll past the house behind which sat the Hallmark Pool, that "A" scouted out and cleaned out by Chili and SP very early in the season. They had lost her midsummer, when a family moved into the previously abandoned house. They showed up one day to ride and the gem was full of water—"It was devastating," SP would later relay to a friend—and little kids were splashing around in the shallow end right next to that smooth pocket that many times had slingshot Chili back into the nearly flawless deep end. Indeed, the Hallmark was a contender for Pool of the Year (up there with a capsule-shaped gem in Ojai and San Diego's Pala Round).

Coasting by the now-occupied house, SP got a glimpse through the side-yard fence. Yep, still full. Oh, well. Worth a look, anyway.

Byron piped up from the back seat: "I swam in that thing, dude"—indeed, he had, on a scorching August day when nobody was home—"I was the only one to swim in it."

TONY CAPALBY CUTS A BACKSIDE LAYBACK OVER THE
LOVE SEAT AT ROSA'S, SPRING 2002
PHOTO: JIM KNIGHT

"No, dude," SP shot back. "TA was swimming that thing waaaay before you even knew how to swim." They all laughed—it had been a long summer of respectfully mocking the egocentric rhetoric spilling from legendary Tony "TA" Alva, the pioneering pool skater and original Zephyr team rider who, true to form, had grandstanded during his segments in both *Dogtown and Z-Boys* and *Fruit of the Vine*, the more underground instant classic pool-skating documentary by New York–based filmmakers Coan "Buddy" Nichols and Rick Charnoski.

They'd barely finished busting up when Chili pulled to the curb across the street from Rosa's, a sort-of kidney-shaped bowl built by Swan Pools and named after the stern yet generous *abuelita* who, along with three generations of immediate family, lived in a typical three-bedroom suburban home backed up to a long alley. With a twelve-pack of Bud Light longnecks, Chili walked alone to the front door, knocked, and was greeted by one of the teenage grandchildren, who, with incredible hospitality, unlocked the side-yard gate and invited everybody through. Chili said thanks as she turned back inside to deliver the twelver to her grandfather.

TO BE SURE, CHILI AND CREW have always deployed every pool-hunting technique available. Many searching techniques come naturally, such as interrogating neighborhood skater kids or offering to trade pool whereabouts with other skateboarders. Arguably the best technique, but out of reach financially, would have Chili and crew flying rented planes and helicopters over entire regions. A few approaches have even been spelled out in skateboard magazines by pool skaters who, it could be argued, should have known better than to divulge such clever tricks of the clandestine trade. For example, when *Thrasher* published legendary Inland Empire pool skater Steve "Salba" Alba's pool-skating article that suggested skaters scan the federal government's Housing and Urban Development real estate list, Chili did just that, and soon uncovered a few empty bowls. None of these techniques, however, led Chili to Rosa's.

He came across Rosa's the old-fashioned way, the way it's been done since the beginning: Find an alley, put a man on the roof of the car, and drive slowly enough to allow him a good look into every backyard. After they had first spotted Rosa's—at that time a few feet deep in green water—they had rolled around to the front door and knocked. A teenage boy and girl had answered, and Chili explained that he was making a movie about skateboarding and was scouting locations to shoot some pool-skating footage (indeed, he was, and it would by summer's end become a grainy, no-budget masterpiece of skating, music, and humor entitled *Fart Sandwich* and handed out only to his closest friends). The kids had gone to get Grandma Rosa, who looked Chili up and down sternly before listening to his story through the kids' translation.

After a solid five minutes of smiling and being very, very nice, Chili was allowed into the backyard to take a closer look at the pool. At last given the thumbs-up, Chili had called on the rest to unload the buckets, brooms, old towels, dustpans, and gas-powered pool pump piled in the back of his van. If they had had a box of Milkbone doggie biscuits, they would have fed a few to Shadow, the family dog, if only to keep the slobbering, yelping black Labrador quiet while they worked. Forty minutes later, she was dry, but the sun was on its way down, and Chili figured the family had gone through enough ruckus for the day, so they decided to return the following week for her inaugural

HEY, STEVE ALBA. I SAW YOUR GLOSSY, FLY, FUCKING, YOU KNOW, LAYOUT, DUDE, IN *TRANSWORLD*. YOU KNOW WHO THIS IS? IT'S TONY ALVA, DUDE, AND I'M NOT DIGGING YOUR FUCKING OVEREXPOSURE OF POOLS. I NEVER RIDE YOUR FUCKING POOLS. I DON'T EVER ASK YOU WHAT THE FUCK IS GOING. BUT YOU'RE GIVING OUT THE SECRETS, DUDE. "SALBA'S POOL-FINDING TIPS"? DUDE, THAT SHIT IS WACK. YOU'RE FUCKING TRIPPING, DUDE, BIG TIME. ESPECIALLY WHEN YOU'RE SWEATING MY HOMEBOYS FOR FUCKING EVEN COMING TO RIDE YOUR SHIT. I'M PISSED OFF. YOU FUCKING CALL ME UP. LET'S TALK ABOUT IT, DUDE. CUZ THERE AIN'T NO POOL-FINDING TIPS FOR NOBODY, EXCEPT YOU AND ME. AND YOU'RE FUCKING SPREADING THE WORD? WHAT'S UP WITH THAT, DUDE? FUCK, DUDE, THAT AIN'T RIGHT. FROM DAY ONE, DUDE, '77, '75, '74, '73, I GO BACK TO WHEN YOU WERE IN FUCKING DIAPERS, DUDE. DON'T FUCKING THROW DOWN NO POOL FUCKING INFO LIKE THAT. THAT AIN'T COOL, DUDE
TONY ALVA'S MESSAGE ON STEVE ALBA'S PHONE MACHINE, SUMMER 2000

session. Not bad, they concluded, grading her in the mid- to high 80s, all in all a solid B, with bonus points for being a permission.

Rosa's had been going all season, and like surfers who religiously ride the glassy sets just before sundown, Chili and crew had made a summer ritual of glassing off Rosa's with a twelve-pack of their own. She was a great bowl for an evening-glass session. Aside from being a permission, Rosa's was also a fun bowl with lots of deep-end obstacles—two love seats, a light, and a deathbox—best attacked after plenty of warm-up.

After a four-pool warm-up, the attacks started early as the day faded to a warm late afternoon. Beers were cracked. Tony drew pretzel lines over both love seats, carving over the left love backside and tightening his line to wrap himself back over the right love without ever leaving the deep end. SP scraped the polished-pebble coping over the right love seat with both trucks backside before two shallow-wall hits sent him back into the deep, where he threaded between the light and left love to let her have it frontside.

And Chili, on one of his last backyard pool days in California before shoving off to his new job in Hawaii, drew a brand-new line frontside over the left love and sucked it in, just missing the face-wall light, standing through it like he'd done it his whole life, stoking a few hoots from the shallow.

Kresky rolled a cigarette. A flock of cockatiels flapped overhead. Shadow stopped barking long enough to whizz on the half-empty twelver. Long shadows grew across the Southland, and the crew kept at it until darkness finally chased away the sun. Sweaty and comfortably sore, they thanked Rosa and her family before climbing back into Chili's van. On the way to their favorite dive bar for rounds of Bud and farewell shots of Hornitos, Chili kept his eyes peeled, staring down every empty home, making mental notes of yet untapped alleys, always searching for the Holy Grail, that elusive 99.

4 THE '70s
(THE NATURAL

ON GOOD DAYS, JAY ADAMS IS UP BEFORE THE SUN.

HE SELECTS A SURFBOARD FROM HIS QUIVER, RESTS IT GENTLY IN THE BED OF HIS '65 FORD STEPSIDE, AND CRUISES KAM HIGHWAY ALONG OAHU'S

NORTH SHORE.
Shoulders thick from decades of paddling, eyes as blue and clear as the tropical Pacific, deeply tanned from shaved head to callused feet, Jay looks healthy, belying his forty-two years. As dawn rises, he's checking out world-famous Pipeline, a tremendously fast-throwing reef break. Set waves are double overhead. Pipeline's Backdoor—one of Jay's favorite waves—is breaking cleanly. Daybreak backlights the mountain jungle. The breeze whispers offshore. Jay paddles out and greets a few friends in the lineup. A set approaches and he's scratching for the peak. In an instant he's up and surfing down the smooth face of a mountainous, moving wall of water. It jacks up, pitching its heavy lip over and down, and Jay slides loosely into a high-speed tube ride until the warm and salted crush of the collapsing barrel on his heels spits him to the wave shoulder. Dropping prone, he paddles back to the lineup.

As the morning warms, Jay surfs—barrel after spitting barrel—until he's tired and hungry and catches one to the sand. Cruising into Haleiwa with one eye on the road, the other on the blue Pacific, he takes a seat outside at Cholo's and orders a broad plate of spicy huevos rancheros. After breakfast, he surfs again, jogs, or lift weights at home. On his doorstep, a large box holds several pairs of his signature skateboard shoes, and there's also fan mail from a pretty Latina who's enclosed a Polaroid of her curvaceous bosom. If there's an empty swimming pool to be had, Jay lines up a session with the men who hold the key, Gary Owens and Grant Fukuda. Or he heads toward Diamond Head with Steve Ellis to ride the public skatepark in Hawaii Kai. Later that afternoon, he's getting naked with his gal. They surf the evening glass together. Come suppertime, he's back at Cholo's or cooking a steak at home. Overcome with the deep ache of satisfying physical exhaustion, Jay hits the sack pretty early.

On bad days, Jay's tightly wound, nervous and twitching with energy. He can't sit still. The waves are down and blown out. The only empty pool going is a steep and deadly pitfall. Hawaii Kai's smooth concrete and steel coping are slick from sporadic downpours: hardly worth the drive through Honolulu's rush hour. His girlfriend is away on a trip and not checking in; heartbreaking scenarios rage in his idle mind. He wonders what to do. He's bored. He's antsy. He's not wired for this, a life without adrenaline, without rush

and risk. Soon he's hanging out with good friends with bad habits, friends who smoke ice, the crack version of crystal meth. Other friends try to find him. But he's MIA.

A day passes, then a night. He reappears, eyes glazed over. Jay looks tired. He's giving away what's left of a batch of powerful muscle relaxants. He's jonesing for surf, itching to skate, and he's nervous about a pending meeting with his parole officer. A few days later, Jay is

facing the music. And it's hurting his ears. He just pissed dirty, but he swears up and down to his P.O. that he hasn't touched shit, that the drug test must be wrong. He pisses again. This time it's negative—Jay isn't going back to jail. Back home, his friend Ellis warns him: "I keep telling you, man, you can either be in jail without drugs, or you can be out of jail without drugs. It's a pretty easy choice, I would think."

FORTUNATELY FOR JAY, his good days far outnumber his bad. Used to be the other way around, however—and not too long ago—when hard drugs, particularly heroin, tore him down and dictated his decisions.

Jay was going through a rough one: in the mid-'90s, four of his immediate family died and a girlfriend left him. The tragedy's first act unfolded when drug dealers murdered Jay's half-brother, Anthony Romero, for sixty thousand dollars and a kilo of cocaine. Within the year, Jay's grandmother had died of cancer and his father (by blood) had headed off his own cancer with a suicidal dose of pills. His grandmother's and father's deaths, Jay says, didn't affect him terribly because he wasn't close to them. But then his mother, Philaine Romero, was diagnosed with cancer. At the time, Jay was living in Santa Cruz with the mother of his son, but it wasn't working out, so he moved back to Hawaii. His dying mother soon followed. As her caretaker, Jay was in charge of her pain medication. He started popping her pills. When the bottle was empty, he'd order enough for them both. The opiates made him feel good, numbing the pain of watching cancer take ten months to devour his mother.

After his mother died, Jay battled and ignored his depression with a comforting island life. He lived near

JAY WAS A STANDOUT FROM THE MOMENT YOU FIRST SAW HIM. IN THE EARLY DAYS, NOBODY COULD COMPARE TO HIM. SKATEBOARDING WAS MOVING BY LEAPS AND BOUNDS, AND JAY WAS THE MOST PROGRESSIVE, JUST PUSHING IT, GOING FOR IT
GLEN E. FRIEDMAN, PHOTOGRAPHER

IF JAY WASN'T PUSHING HIS LIFE TO THE LIMIT AND JUST BARELY SQUEAKING BY ON THE SKIN OF HIS ASS, HE WOULDN'T BE JAY. AND JAY IS JAY

STEVE ELLIS

Sunset—one of the finest waves on the planet—with a girlfriend and his boy, Seven (who was four at the time), surfed every day, repaired dinged surfboards, and went to church on Sundays. He also sold dope on the side; the extra income enhanced the good life. But then he started smoking his profits. His addiction got out of hand. The good life took a dive. Jay's girlfriend moved to the opposite side of the island, fading from contact. Jay suspected she was seeing someone new. One morning, he left Seven with the babysitter and dropped in on his girl unannounced, finding the woman he loved in bed with another guy. Jay mixed it up with them both, slapping her and scrapping with the stranger before the cops arrived. Jay went to jail, trapped by jealous rage and sadness. The camel's back had broken.

Once free, he dove back into drugs with a renewed fervor for self-destruction. Putting down the pipe, he tried shooting heroin for the first time, a fix that shoved him over a rapidly crumbling edge. Jay was gone. Falling from the top of his father's priority list, Seven stayed with the babysitter until his mom flew out and took him back to Santa Cruz. Jay slipped deeper. Arrested for burglary and threatening to kill a man, he faced hard time but walked with five years' probation. Soon thereafter, while crashing at a drug dealer's house, he was searched during an early-morning raid. The cops found a bindle in his wallet. Sent to prison, *haole* Jay was surrounded by hardened thugs who hated whitey. Serving two and a half years of an open ten-year sentence in three Hawaiian prisons, Jay

had plenty of time to learn to hate them right back. He also earned his high school diploma.

While Jay was doing hard time, his former fellow skateboarder from the mid-'70s, Stacy Peralta, was overseeing the creation of the hit 2002 documentary *Dogtown and Z-Boys*. The award-winning film chronicles the rise and fall of the Zephyr skateboard team— Tony Alva, Bob Biniak, Chris Cahill, Paul Constantineau, Shogo Kubo, Jim Muir, Peggy Oki, Nathan Pratt, Wenzel Ruml, Allen Sarlo, Peralta, and Jay—whose loose, low-slung riding style and aggressive delivery signaled a paradigm shift from the upright and technically gymnastic trick book held over from skateboarding's original mid-'60s surge. Once it was released, *Dogtown*'s edgy nostalgia quickly elevated Jay to the pedestals he had avoided back when the Z-Boys were in their prime. Many in the skateboard world wondered: When is Jay getting out of prison, and will he make a mainstream comeback? Behind bars, Jay entertained offers from skateboard and shoe companies wanting to move product on the building swell of his mythical name. The pendulum swung, the roller coaster climbed, and Jay's life again held promise.

Jay's whole life, like anybody's life, has been a series of climbs and plunges. But with Jay, the ride's been more extraordinary on each end. The highs are higher and the lows lower: from the peaks, he harvests heaven; from the valleys, he dredges hell. And to say his soul has not been tortured by this incessant rise and dive is to say Jay is not human.

BORN ON FEBRUARY 3, 1961, the only child of Robert Adams and Philaine Romero, Jay Adams lost his heroin-addict father to prison while still a baby.

JAY ADAMS, VENICE BEACH, CIRCA 1989
PHOTO COURTESY OF
KEVIN SOARES

ADAMS
JAY
S#:   175671
Height: 507
Weight: 160
Sex: M
Race: WHITE
DOA: 08 / 15 / 1995
DOB: 02 / 03 / 61

Released years later, Robert made contact with nine-year-old Jay but would never reenter his life. Fortunately for young Jay, his mother went to a Venice party one night in 1964 and met Kent Sherwood. A lifelong surfer born and raised on Oahu, Kent had moved to California in 1962 and for two years had glassed surfboards for well-known shapers Dave Sweet and Greg Noll before opening Plastic Works, where he solved problems and fabricated prototypes for artists and engineers. In 1965, with four-year-old Jay under his wing, Kent opened a beach concession—renting boards, mats, chairs, and umbrellas—in the northern shadows of the Pacific Ocean Pier. "Jay rode surf mats for a while," Kent remembers. "When he got used to the water, I made him a little surfboard. He caught on real quick . . . a natural. He took to the water like a duck."

On Kent's busy days, local surfers—most of whom skateboarded when the waves were down—looked after young Jay, and before his fifth birthday, he was bronzed by the blessed existence of a Southern California beach life. Indeed, Jay doesn't remember a time when he wasn't already surfing and skateboarding. "P.O.P. [Pacific Ocean Park] was my playground," Jay says. "I ran around and went on all the amusement rides for free, knew all the guards, and I learned to surf at the Cove and Ts and all that. It was just a big playground that was given to me by my stepfather. I owe it all to him because he was a surfer, and back then surfing and skateboarding went hand in hand."

Though Kent and Philaine would never marry, Jay refers to him as his stepfather, and Kent raised Jay like a son. When Jay refused to read in school, Kent bought him a stack of *Surfer* magazines; Jay read them cover to cover, particularly captivated by the articles on and photos of Hawaii. As Jay grew more confident and skilled in larger surf, Kent loaded up Jay and his friends and headed down Mexico way for long weekend surf safaris south of Ensenada, or maybe up the Pacific Coast Highway to ride Rincon or Oxnard beach breaks. Through skateboarding's late-'60s down days, when it was nearly impossible to find a board for sale, Kent and Jay built skateboard decks from lumberyard oak, finishing off the custom planks with

ADAMS
JAY
S#:   175671
Height: 507
Weight: 160
Sex: **M**
Race: **WHITE**
DOA: 06 / 24 / 1998
DOB: 02 / 03 / 61

SOME OF THE DARKEST CHARACTERS IN THIS WORLD ARE ACTUALLY VERY SCARED AND OPERATE OUT OF FEAR AND USE ALL THESE PROPS, LIKE TATTOOS, RACIAL SLURS, BAD LANGUAGE, AND AN UNKEMPT APPEARANCE, BECAUSE IT HELPS KEEP PEOPLE AWAY FROM THEM, AND I THINK JAY HAS A LITTLE BIT OF THAT GOING ON. . . . DOWN DEEP, JAY IS REALLY A FUNNY AND COOL GUY. HE HAS HAD A HARD LIFE, AND, YES, HE IS RESPONSIBLE FOR CREATING MOST OF IT, BUT HE IS TRYING TO DO THE RIGHT THING. HE HASN'T GIVEN UP

DAVE HACKETT, PRO

holdover trucks and clay wheels. When seas flattened, Kent drove the boys to Palisades High, where Jay would bomb the sloping parking lot all afternoon. No shoes, no grip tape, just a kid cutting surf carves across smooth asphalt. "Pali High," Jay remembers. "In the old days, that was where the Hobie skate team used to go. Just a big, long, beautiful parking lot that you could go back and forth in. Skateboarding back then was copying surfing. So, when you go downhill back and forth on clay wheels, you're just pretending you're surfing."

Closer to home, Jay attacked countless skate spots all over town. Directly in front of his house was a curb on which he'd practice his cutbacks. Across the street was a steep driveway drop he called Pipeline. Down the road was a fast plunge through an apartment complex; he called that one Waimea. Right next door was Sunset. And anywhere he found shrubbery overhanging the sidewalk, Jay would tuck into a "bush barrel."

In the water, as on the concrete, Jay rose through the ranks like a prodigy, influenced by P.O.P. Pier's South

Side Surfers' fierce localism and high-performance drive in the water. Defending their waves from outsiders, Jay and the rest of the upcoming generation of surfer-skaters—many of whom later joined the Zephyr team—pelted kooks with rocks and bottles and rotten fruit. They slashed tires, smashed windshields, and decorated sea walls and benches with spray-painted warnings: "Locals only," "Death to invaders," "Vals go home." In the water they surfed with a style to match their aggressive territorialism. And, most important, they learned to stay on. P.O.P. Pier had crumbled into economic blight in the late '6os, and at the Cove in particular, the break was littered with the jagged-steel and snapped-piling remains of the famed Coney Island of the West. One wrong move and a fallen surfer could crack his skull, end up impaled, or both.

After their morning surf, they took their moves to the massive banks behind neighboring schoolyards—Paul Revere Junior High and Kenter Canyon, Bellagio, Brentwood, and Mar Vista elementary schools—driven by one mantra: surf to skate, skate to surf. They also began barging backyard pools, taking their bank maneuvers to the vertical walls behind the rich homes in Santa Monica, Brentwood, Beverly Hills, and Pacific Palisades, slow-rolling through countless alleys, always on the hunt for new bowls. Aided and abetted by one of the worst droughts on California record, they mainly skated bone-dry bowls. Other pools, however, sat half-filled with green muck, and many still shimmered with chlorine-clear water—for these they came prepared with pumps, buckets, brooms, and old towels. Kent bought Jay his first pool pump.

By the time Jay was a teenager, his life moved mellifluously between the seemingly disparate worlds of saltwater and concrete, and his future was set: he'd be a surfer and a skateboarder. His attitude too had taken hold: he could not be bothered by much else beyond the endless thrill and utter joy bestowed by two boards, one with fins, the other with wheels. Even before his tenth birthday, Jay was bagging trophies in surf contests—he was soon ranked number one in the World Surfing Association's boys' division—but he quickly learned that such competition meant little. He didn't like people telling him when and where to surf and for how long. During one contest, Kent remembers, Jay surfed exceptionally through a qualifying round, chalking up a series of high-scoring rides. But when his heat ended, Jay refused to turn his back on great waves. As blaring bullhorns called the surfers to shore, Jay stayed out and kept riding. He also refused to let studying detract from his bliss. Early in high school, Jay had an understanding principal who let him earn P.E. credits in the water, and he didn't have to show up for class until midmorning. But by the time tenth grade rolled around, Jay had dropped out entirely, finding his playmates while surfing and skating or down at the surf shop.

Located one mile north of P.O.P., on the corner of Bay and Main streets, the Jeff Ho & Zephyr Productions surf shop had been open since 1972, when surfboard shapers Ho, twenty-three, and Skip Engblom, twenty-four, and artist Craig Stecyk III, twenty-one, diverted from surfing's flowery mainstream to launch a line unique to Venice, drawing from a cultural palette of hot rods and low-riders, vatos and Latinas. They also compiled a team of the best surfers and skateboarders in Dogtown, a territory encompassing South Santa Monica, Venice, and Ocean Park. (With Jay's input, Kent designed and fabricated Zephyr's first skateboard, a fiberglass ride modeled after a '6os shape produced by Hobie.) Many of the surfers from Zephyr's junior surf team, Jay included, comprised the first and only Z-Boy skateboard team,

NEXT:
JAY ADAMS BARRELING AT BACKDOOR, NORTH SHORE, HAWAII, LATE WINTER 2003
PHOTO: DAVE BJORN

JAY'S MAIN THING IN LIFE WAS SURFING. IT'S ALL HE WANTED TO DO. SURFING WAS ALL THAT MATTERED. HE COULDN'T MAKE IT THROUGH HIGH SCHOOL. I KINDA BLAME MYSELF FOR THAT. YOU KNOW, IT'S TOO BAD. HE COULD'VE BEEN ANYTHING HE WANTED TO BE. BUT THAT'S WHAT HE WANTED TO BE, A SURFER. SO WHAT CAN I SAY?

KENT SHERWOOD

a street-tough surf-rat pack of mainly broken-home hellions whose lots in life seemed to be dead-ends, but who were also genetically drawn to the open spaces of their vast proving grounds: the Pacific Ocean and the concrete sprawl of Southern California.

For Jay, those open spaces now extended to the tropics. As he remembers, he first set foot on Hawaii in the early '70s on a trip with Kent. "The first thing I did . . . I went and I had to touch the water because my step-dad told me how warm it was. It was the biggest moment in my life. Hawaii's just the ultimate of surfing, whether it's town or the North Shore. When you're a kid, you dream about coming to Hawaii. At least I did. That was my biggest dream in the world."

WITH THE INTRODUCTION of Frank Nashworthy's urethane wheel in 1973, skateboarding cut its umbilical link to surfing. To be sure, the Z-Boys' influences were purely surfing-based—their hairpin cutbacks, a laid-out sliding pivot around the leading hand, were called Berts after the famed Hawaiian surfer Larry Bertelman—but the smooth grip and glide of urethane wheels (Cadillacs were the first) gave all skateboarders new direction, traction, and potential. Delivered from the ocean's womb, skateboarding grew into its own. Combined, this overnight advance in speed and maneuverability and the Z-Boys' aggressive knack for banked and vertical riding pushed skateboarding into a whole new realm. Jay's clarification: "The *Dogtown* movie tries to come off like we were the first . . . and we weren't. We weren't the first to skate pools. There were guys skating pools in the '60s, too, and there were other guys, like from Playa del Rey, that were skating pools after they tore down all those houses. [They] were skating pools at the same time [we were]. But with the new equipment and stuff, we definitely took it to a new level. And it became an obsession for us where all we wanted to do was ride pools. And we had a little advantage because we had been riding banks at Paul Revere and stuff, so we had a feeling for transition already."

By 1975, when Jay was fourteen, the skateboard industry had regained its footing. Bahne, the leading manufacturer of boards and wheels at the time, hosted the biggest contest since the '60s. During Bahne's Del Mar nationals, as *Dogtown and Z-Boys* depicts, "The Z-Boys took skateboarding's traditional upright approach and drove it right into the ground." Soon thereafter, skateboarding's popularity surged massively. Talented teams formed. Cutting-edge decks, wheels, and trucks flooded the market (along with countless useless gimmicks). Skateparks cropped up across the nation. Contests made the airwaves. Bigger companies coaxed Dogtown's most talented skateboarders, Jay included, away from their home shop, and the Zephyr team disbanded within six months of the contest.

JASON I wrote you probably two letters that you might not have gotten. Cause I think they said you'd gone to LA during that time. And if you didn't go back to work after that then you probably didn't get them. Plus I never got any mail from you either. So if you sent it something went wrong cause I never even got a PINK SLIP. So what's up? Are you over the consolidated deal? let me know what's going on. And what your plans are. If you're not gonna go back to them and you wanna still do something in the SKATEBOARD world I wanna do 100% skateboarder And you'd be a perfect guy to help me. I MEAN I don't know if you already got something going but it's AN IDEA! My last letter to you I asked you to look into getting the NAME for me. I want to just start with a few Shirts But i think Decks and the whole other deal could follow.

I cant think of anybody else who even deserves to be a part of it than you I think the NAME SAYS it all. And I'm sure we could put together a team. Plus if we got it going I would give me another reason to move back to Cali to be closer to my boy.

But even if your gonna be a plummer or a cook at a restaurant can you help me still by checking out if i can get the name. Karma has wrote me a few times And he mentioned something about Consolidated getting a little money hungry, well I personally don't think there's anything wrong with making some money, as long as you Don't turn Homo to have to do it.

○ yeah thax For take some time to spend with my boy and For the skate Yesterday plus you might not have much his life

Well I never made much. But I plan on trying my best to make a living on the business side of skateboarding. If I was a kid I'd rather ride for a guy like me or you than some John Falahee or Rocko type. Well maybe rocko has a lot to offer but let's face it he's always been a Freestyle FAG. And I plan on making room For myself in their world. Whatever bro You know I gotta have something to dream about when I get outta here. And having my own company doesn't seem very impossible at all. I wanna have a team of guys. And take em all over on skate trips and shit.

Well I found out I gotta do level 2 not level 3 substance abuse so that's the diffrance of 1 yr. I still gotta do my time but level 3 is pretty intence compared to level 2 so im pretty happy about this. I could finish level 2 in 4 to 6 months and then go to LAMAKA work Furlow after that shit hamma. Lamaka is out already I'll be working At BLACK FLY in WAIKIKI so i could actually be doing whatever skate buisness from their. So DID I tell you? ○○○

Q) whats the diffrance between Martin luther King and Rodney King?
A) MLK had a dream, Rodney had a NIGHT MARE
Q) How do you get the nigger outta the tree in MISSISSIPPI?
A) Cut the ROPE

OK you me and Karma all died and had to stand befor God he asked us if we ever cheated on our wives So First he asked Karma and Karma said yes lord i cheated on my wife over 100 times the lord said ok Karma for being truthful im going to give you this car to drive around in heaven it was a rusted out 64 NOVA Then he asked you if you're ever cheated on you wife you said yes lord I cheated on my wife At least 5 times And the lord said oK

Jaso for telling the truth heres A 95 Bmw to drive in heaven So then the lord asked me if I ever cheated on my wife I said Lord I never cheated on my wife lord And he said Very Good Jay For telling the truth im giving you this brand new rolls royce to drive in heaven. So me you and Karma were in my rolls royce driving Around And when we stopped At the Light I started crying. And you guys said what are you crying For Jay you got A rolls royce And I said See that Lady in the SKATEboard sled's my WIFE. (some related shit?)

Hey I just got a letter from Fletcher it doesn't say much And I also got a note saying something Didn't make it through that he sent. but it doesn't say what.

→ 5 min Book to get mail → I talked to the people at Joice. they still WANNA do your Interview. they I Also got my eye opperation they cut my eyeball and threw put stitches in it. That shit hurt like hell for the first 2 days. CAN you ASK VANS if they will Send my boy Some Shoes? Also I WAS wondering if they would do A Shoe for me copy the Converse one Chuck trayler style but change the logo to MIron cross's I Don't think it would hurt to ASK since you know the guys maybe you could mention it. Also STACY never mentioned Any money From VANS for the DECO. he said he did it outta love And didn't make Any money For himself. He's in the Sundance Film Festival So if it makes Any money maybe they might Kick down Something later. I feel I have even Asking about shit like this I think I have Ego phobia or something But if you never ASK you'll never know if it could have been right. Any way that's it write me back fuck free i don't like callin your huse cause it will cost you money

I never mentioned money i'm sorry either.

I that the SHOES

IAZy Boy ELLI counting Down

SANTA CRUZ 13
100% SKATEBOARDER

FUCK THE AMERICAN DREAM

RIDE SKATEBOARDS

Funner than crack More Addictive than Heroin $$$ And its Almost legal

100% SKATEBOARDER

ROCKO this one of Aning money

I'd rather SKATE THAN FUCK

Say skateing away from crying girl

BACK Jersey style 13 on Front

BLACK & white

SORRY I'M not AN Artist Just some IDEAS

Jay was in his prime, to be sure, but he didn't let it go to his head. Unmotivated by fame, unrestrained by convention, outstandingly innovative, supremely spontaneous, and sufficiently crazy, Jay was the skateboarder's skateboarder. And his skill kept growing, fueled by the advantages of the sponsored skateboarder. Free equipment. Free admission to any skatepark. Free trips to contests, skatepark openings, and parking-lot demonstrations in front of thousands. And Jay just had to keep doing what he'd always done: skateboarding and surfing with his friends on a daily basis. The good life was getting better. Kent enjoyed it, too: "We'd go out at Malibu, at the pier, and as I'm getting ready to take off on a wave, I could hear people yelling at others, 'Don't take off! Don't take off! That's Jay's dad!,' which was kinda nice."

Jay's status soared. Promoters and sponsors, magazine editors and moviemakers, grommets and groupies all wanted a piece of whatever it was he had, or they wanted to make money off it. For the most part, Jay dodged the spotlight, especially after he learned the hard way that many promises are hollow. When he didn't get burned, however, he managed to pull down enough from endorsements to help his mom with rent before escaping to the tropics on extended surf trips, often alone. He'd return deeply tanned, relaxed, and clear-headed, itching to skate, and slip right back into his routine of surfing in the morning, skating Marina del Rey's skatepark or a backyard pool until the sun went down, and drinking beer and smoking pot into the night with his best friends.

Magazines of the era referred to him as "unrestrainable," "irrepressible," "a radical little rat," "one radical mutha," and "insanity on wheels." On and off his board, throughout the '70s, Jay's exploits were legendary. Highlights include: booted from the beach for beaning a Santa Monica lifeguard in the head with an orange; busted for skating on the freeway; kicked out of Reseda skatepark more times than he can remember for breaking the "no getting out of control" rule;

A LOT OF TIMES IN POOL SESSIONS, IT DOESN'T MATTER WHO'S AT THE SESSION, IT'S ALWAYS DICTATED BY THE PERSON WHO IS MOST SPONTANEOUS. I MEAN, TONY ALVA HAD GREAT STYLE, BUT IF THERE WASN'T JAY ADAMS, THEN TONY ALVA, I MEAN, I DON'T KNOW . . .
MARK GONZALES, PRO

getting chased through a Mexico City brothel by a lactating hooker; snatching old ladies' wigs as he skated past; shocking strangers with the large swastikas painted on his skateboards; instigating food fights of epic proportions; and leaving a wake of vandalism as he skated down the sidewalk, slamming his board into every parked car with each cutback. His soundtrack? "I skate at maximum when I'm in a pool with my friends with some loud music going," Jay told Stan Sharp for the December 1977 issue of *Skateboard World*. "Preferably Hendrix, Nugent, ZZ Top, or Zeppelin. Under such conditions anything is possible." Life was good, a heady mix of concrete and saltwater laced with sex, drugs, and rock and roll.

By the end of the '70s, however, "things got lame," Jay says. "I got pretty anti-contest and all that. I didn't like to be told what to do and how to do it. And it just started looking fuckin' gay after a while, like all the little Pepsi teams and fuckin' going to skateparks and you gotta wear fuckin' wrist guards and shit. I was fuckin' over that shit. And a lot of guys who I was hanging out with, just their egos got out of control, and it fuckin' looked stupid to me. And it wasn't just the guys I was hanging out with. Like we'd go to a skatepark and guys would fuckin' follow you around all day trying to fuckin' outdo you and shit. Everybody had an ego trip. It wasn't as fun as it always was once it became so professional. And I always thought ego was the biggest poison."

DESPITE PERALTA'S EULOGISTIC treatment in *Dogtown and Z-Boys*, Jay Adams did not die suddenly at the end of his skateboarding career in the late '70s. He simply slipped farther out of the spotlight's fringes. "Actually," he remembers, "for about a year I wasn't skating too much. I was hanging out with Mexican guys in Venice. Probably [in] '79, '78, I started hanging out with these low-rider guys, and we had a little gang called the Venice Hoodlums. I definitely got the cholo influence, wearing khakis and all that shit. Pendletons. And I was just more into fuckin' causing trouble and getting drunk and smoking dust and fuckin' trying to make people fear me.

"Then I got into that punk shit, [but at first] I thought punk rock was like Devo and Talking Heads and shit, and I was like, 'Fuckin' punk is lame, dude,' because I didn't know what the real shit was. Then I [saw] a pretty rad show in Hollywood. . . . I think it was Black Flag, Circle Jerks, Fear, and X. . . . They had a riot and stuff, and after that I was hooked on it. Brainwashed completely. I found out what it was all about. . . . And punk was good for skateboarding because fuckin' skateboarding was getting really soft and fuckin' too organized and controlled. And when punk came around, it was like, 'Fuck the rules. Don't tell us what to do. Fuck authority. Fuck whatever.'"

The '80s dawned and the skateboard industry dove as parks closed and most kids moved on to the next cool thing. Jay remembers that era with a smirk. "Those were fine times for me. I just fuckin' sold weed and shit and still skated and surfed every day. Nothing really changed." That is, until his reputation as an instigator caught up with him.

Jay was running with a group of devoted, Dogtown-based hellraisers who called themselves the Suicidal Boys, and punk rock, specifically the sounds of Venice's Suicidal Tendencies, provided their anthem. "Punk rock back then was going out and beating people up," Jay remembers. "It was violent, and at the time I was into violence. I used to like to go out and ruin people's nights. I was a kid. I had things to prove. I had to fuck someone's night up for me to have a good night." One night in Hollywood, deep into booze and backed by his boys, Jay mouthed off to a male couple—one white, one black—strolling hand in hand down the street. After Jay's initial provocation—"Fuck you, you fuckin' homos!"—things got ugly.

"I kicked the big white guy, knocked him into the paper machines . . . and then the black guy squared off and I took off my shirt and I go, 'Come on! Nigger! Faggot! I'll kill you!' And he socked me. Pow! Knocked me down. Then Polar Bear [Dennis Agnew] knocked him out. Boom! Then the white guy came back over, and I ran and I jumped and kicked him in the mouth and knocked him out. So they were both on the ground, basically knocked out. And I grabbed Dennis and we left. . . . A bunch of [other] guys started kicking the black guy, with boots on. And he died. I didn't think he died. I mean, we drove around the block and saw the ambulances, and I was like, 'Whoa, that's pretty gnarly.' So we went home, thought, 'Beat up some homos. No big deal. Just another night. We do that shit all the time.' And [a few days] later, I hear a knock and I look out and there's like ten cops. And I was like, 'Holy shit!' I ran and hid . . . in my closet. They found me."

The cops also found a bloodstained shirt on which Jay had written "black man's blood" and drawn an arrow pointing to the stain. But it was from an earlier event, Jay explained. "There was this car accident and these three black guys ran into this wall, and they were all fucked up, and I helped. I pulled one of them out, and he bled on me."

The cops read Jay his rights and took him in. They had picked up Agnew, too. Both were booked for murder. Kent posted bail and hired an attorney, who got the charges reduced. Jay was out of jail within six months.

Jay's heyday as a professional skateboarder faded, but he continued skating throughout much of Southern California and chasing waves across the South Pacific, his life an endless summer. In 1982, *Thrasher* put him

"Hawaii's home," he says.

Mythologized by a generation drawn to dark heroes, and blackened with tattoos—from portraits of Mickey Dora, Duke Paoa Kahanamoku, Charles Manson, and Adams's mother to the indelibly etched "Menace to Society," "White Pride," and "Venice Hoodlums"—Jay Adams is nonetheless approachable, noticeably polite, and absolutely sincere. And though he may have done countless things to prove otherwise, those who know him best say he's exceptionally intelligent. They also call him trustworthy, honest, and a true man of the moment, wherever that moment may take him, for better or worse.

At his worst, Jay Adams is a felon, a junkie, and a racist and homophobic deadbeat dad. At his best, he's

PUNK ROCK SAVED SKATEBOARDING

JAY ADAMS

on a cover carving a Dogtown street for Craig Stecyk's camera. Published rumor describes him jumping off the end of the Santa Monica pier to surf monstrous waves during the El Niño swell of 1983. And for the January 1989 issue, *Thrasher* put him on the cover again, this time frontside-grinding an egg-shaped backyard pool above a tagline reading, "Skateboarding is . . ." Inside, the cover's caption states, "With punishing elegance, the elusive and intrusive master of the abusive Jay Adams harsh grinds the Egg Bowl. . . ."

Clearly, Jay's legacy had endured.

A DOZEN YEARS LATER, his harshest years behind him, Jay's blessed with a boy and living on Oahu's North Shore, where he's hung his hat off and on since the early '70s.

a legendary surfer and skateboarder, an honest and sober guy who goes to church on Sundays and sends his kid money each month. And if he keeps surfing and skateboarding, like he's done since before he can remember, Jay will always be known not for what he does worst, but for what he does best.

"The guys I like are the guys who are fuckin' in it for life," he says. "I've just seen too many people come and go—pro for a year or two and then just fuckin' rollerblading the next year, mountain biking or something. People in it for the wrong reasons. I just kind of like the fact that I've been doing it since I was four years old and still do it. I still go out and surf Backdoor Pipeline with all the boys, or I'll go skate a pool with the guys. That's what I've done my whole life. That's what I'm gonna keep doing until I can't do it anymore."

FIVE A.M.

SOMEWHERE IN THE AMERICAN SOUTHWEST, WHERE STIFF WINDS PUSH TRACTOR-SIZED TUMBLEWEEDS

ALONG THE HIGH MESAS, THE STIFF SHRILL OF A WAKEUP PHONE CALL RIPS FIVE SKATEBOARDERS FROM SLEEP.

Eyes bloodshot, they get to their feet slow and mumbling but noticeably spirited, each pulling on several layers of clothing. Hats, beanies, and hoodies all around. Outside, the frozen night assaults them: like inhaling spiky icicles. They quickly split up, piling into a pair of trucks, and leave the fleabag motel behind. No coffee, no breakfast. They follow a dark road, headlights cutting through a thickening fog. Twenty minutes later, the lead truck pulls down a short turnoff to a cul-de-sac parking lot invisible from the main road. They spill out and pull on backpacks stuffed with gear—flashlights, ropes, backup parts and tools for their skateboards, pads, helmets, a black Sharpie pen, Lone Star beer. Skateboards under arms, they powerwalk back to the main road. Only one of them—the one wearing the coal-miner's hard hat with a shining headlamp— knows the way. He's the leader. His friends call him Dusto. The others—Caleb, Cruzo, Ripper, and Slim— follow Dusto into the blackness and fog. They're nervous and surging with anticipation, half exhilarated, half spooked by the promise of what lies ahead.

PREVIOUS:
ALLEN GENTRY, SOMEWHERE IN TEXAS, SEPTEMBER 2002
PHOTO COURTESY OF CARTER DENNIS
NEXT:
"THE 24-FOOTER," SOMEWHERE IN ARIZONA, SPRING 1987
PHOTO: STEVE KEENAN

A mile deeper along the main road, headlights materialize from the inky stillness behind them. Flashlights click off—the skateboarders scatter and hide, hunched down roadside as the car passes without pausing. Unseen, they move again down the pavement until a dirt road spurs off behind a low, locked gate. They duck under the bar, moving quickly and quietly near the shore of a lake. The January sky is moonless, stars shrouded by a blanket of icy fog.

Partway along the dirt road, Dusto eases down a steep embankment, picking his way carefully over chunky boulders that glow red under his headlamp. The others follow. The rattlers stay put, hibernating in their stony lairs as the skateboarders at last reach the edge of a broad concrete spillway, locked behind a towering cyclone fence with a "No Trespassing" sign listing a federal phone number for reporting offenders. Ignoring the warning, Dusto digs through his backpack. Brandishing a pair of linesman pliers, he deftly clips away wire wraps securing the fence's edge to a metal pole. Cuts complete, he peels back a lower corner of the fence, opening a small porthole to a sacred realm. Cruzo hands Dusto a doubled-up rope and it's tied off to the pole. Ripper holds back the freed fence corner as Dusto ducks through. Down the vertical concrete wall Dusto descends the knotted

rope, a drop of about fifteen feet. Ripper follows, then Cruzo, Slim, and Caleb. They're in.

Together, they trudge slowly up the steep spillway and at last into the mouth of one of the finest skateable concrete structures on the face of the planet. Its name an abbreviated bastardization of the closest city's name, this concrete pipe measures twenty-two feet in diameter and is, as Slim puts it, "skatepark smooth." From its mouth, where the pipe meets the spillway, this massive conduit stretches horizontally into the side of the earth, burrowing back several hundred feet to where it bends upward ninety degrees like a gigantic hollow elbow, running toward the sky. In this elbow the winded skateboarders convene, huddled in the frigid black, waiting for dawn.

In the darkness they can't read the writing on the walls: ink-marker records of the initiated; stickers pasted high where only the best have carved; arching wheel marks like sweeping brushstrokes across broad reaches far beyond vertical—altogether marking nearly three decades of skateboarders who have made this pilgrimage. But there's no time for nostalgia—these men are freezing. Dawn's coming later than they expected, its warm rays delayed by the heavy fog. Battling to keep warm, they run in place, pace the pipe, chat idly through frosty breath. Caleb skates a few low turns by flashlight. Slim lies down and goes back to sleep, the cold concrete sucking at the remnants of his body heat.

WHEN DUSTO WAS A KID, just about twelve years old, he saw an old *Thrasher* with Texas skateboard legend John Gibson on the cover, doing a frontside thruster waaay up in the same pipe where Dusto's now freezing his ass off. "I said, 'Wow—I wanna skate that shit,'" he remembers. A decade later, returning from a skate trip through Colorado, Dusto and a buddy, following cryp-

MIKE SMITH, PIPELINE SKATEPARK, UPLAND, CALIFORNIA, MAY 1985
PHOTO: STEVE KEENAN

SOME PEOPLE DON'T LIKE THE IDEA OF SKATING PIPES CUZ THEY THINK OF IT AS JUST BACK AND FORTH, BACK AND FORTH. BUT I THINK OF IT AS A WAVE, LIKE RIDING A BIG WAVE. AND I'VE ALWAYS LIKED TO BE UNDERGROUND IN TUNNELS SINCE I WAS A KID. I HAD THE SEWER TUNNELS DIALED IN MY NEIGHBORHOOD. CRUISING AROUND DOWN THERE. I COULD GO THROUGH 'EM WITHOUT A FLASHLIGHT
PETER HEWITT, PRO

tic directions from some skater who'd ridden the pipe, wandered around for hours before spotting it. "We were like, 'Holy shit! There it is!' And we barged it in the middle of the day. We didn't know any better. The guard was driving around, and there were people everywhere. We rode it for about an hour, then got outta there." Since then, he's skated it half a dozen times, each mission a tightly choreographed act of secrecy.

When he's not planning his next pipe trip, Dusto, twenty-seven, works as a vendor for Hitachi, teaching grunts at Lowe's and Home Depot how to sell power tools, a job that sends him traveling in a company car. On the road, he's always scouting for empty pools and checking leads to rumored pipes. At home in San Antonio, he rides a sixty-two-foot-wide half-pipe lined with a concrete lip, which he poured himself. "When I first started working for Hitachi, I got like a nine-hundred-pound package of tools on my doorstep, just boom! And what I do, everything they send me I take out and use on the weekends when I'm working on my ramp."

Caleb, twenty-eight, grew up on South Padre Island, where the southern spur of Texas digs into Mexico. He started surfing when he was a little kid, riding wind-swell

PIPES
(DESERT LEGEND)

MICKE "MALBA" ALBA, MOUNT BALDY, SUMMER 1988

PHOTO: STEVE KEENAN

STEVE "SALBA" ALBA, "THE 24-FOOTER," SPRING 1987
PHOTO: STEVE KEENAN

I JUST NEED TO SKATE NATURAL TERRAIN, FIRST AND FOREMOST. UNDISCOVERED PIPES KEEP ME INSPIRED. PIPES AND POOLS. ANYTHING WHACK AND NATURAL. OTHER THAN THAT . . . IF IT WAS JUST ALL WAREHOUSE SKATING AND PARKS, FUCK, I WOULD HAVE QUIT A LONG TIME AGO. BUT THERE'S STILL THAT ONE ELEMENT THERE: THAT NATURAL STUFF KEEPS ME GOING

DARREL DELGADO,
LONGTIME POOL/PIPE SKATER

beach break kicked up by Caribbean hurricanes. "Everybody that learns how to surf on the Texas coast usually just rips everywhere else cuz it takes so much to learn how to surf those kinds of waves," he says. "Those waves really suck. You really have to love it to put up with those kinds of waves, but we didn't know any better." Caleb got his first skateboard in the mid-'80s from his best friend's older brother and quickly became part of the virtually nonexistent local skate scene. In 1994, he moved to New York for a little while, then spent five years working and surfing in Mexico's Baja California town of San José del Cabo. Caleb lives in Dallas and works as a foreman for a shipping company. He skateboards mostly with Ripper and Cruzo, who turned him on to pool skating, where, he says, he "felt right at home, hitting walls with different transitions—it's a lot like surfing."

Slim's thirty-seven. He was born in Hawaii, raised in Northern California. Now lives in Austin, works as a carpenter. Been with his woman for nine years, and they have a three-year-old boy named Nashville. They call him Nash for short. About twenty years ago, Slim became a member of the Jaks skateboard team, a Bay Area–born, unsanctioned riot of skaters and musicians with chapters worldwide, sort of like skateboarding's Hell's Angels, but not as hirsute and more into skateboard hockey than Harleys. When he moved to Texas in the mid-'90s, the entire state was home to just one other Jak, Big Boys guitarist Tim Kerr, who now lives a block away. Building numbers, Slim petitioned Ripper, who, after surviving his initiation, became a Jak in early 2002. As part of the ritual, Ripper vowed never to disclose the details of his initiation, but does reveal that it included lots of rum, a squad car, and human feces.

Ripper, thirty-three, lives in Dallas and works at a family-owned shipping company. He's married and has a little boy named Jett. On the side, he runs Texas Pool Sharks on the Web. It's been up since 1998, showcasing a bounty of backyard pools and providing a forum where skateboarders from all over Texas—all over the planet, actually—can communicate and trade information about skate spots. Ripper's word: "I don't blow out any spots. I'm super cautious about that stuff—I never put directions to a pool, and the only pictures I post are of pools that are already history."

PETER HEWITT, QUITO, ECUADOR, FEBRUARY 2000
PHOTO: RHINO

I'VE NEVER GOTTEN INTO THE HANDRAIL THING AT ALL. I'VE ALWAYS BEEN INTO SKATING TRANSITION. ALWAYS LOVED SKATING POOLS, AND JUST GETTING IN A FULL PIPE FOR THAT FIRST TIME. . . . WHEN YOU WALK INTO THE MOUTH OF THE THING, IT'S LIKE WALKING INTO A CATHEDRAL. AND LOOKING ALONG THE SIDE WALLS, YOU CAN SEE WHERE PRETTY MUCH EVERYBODY WHO'S SKATED IT HAS SIGNED THEIR NAME ON THE WALL. AND WHEN YOU START LOOKING AT IT AND THE SUN'S RISING, SHINING ON THE WALL, YOU CAN SEE THE NAMES OF ALL THESE HISTORIC, REALLY RAD SKATERS, GOING BACK TO THE '70S. I WAS JUST REALLY BLOWN AWAY BY THE WHOLE EXPERIENCE

ALLEN GENTRY, TEXAS SKATER

Cruzo, thirty-three, also makes his home in Dallas, and works at a fabrication shop, building race cars from scratch. Been skateboarding for about fifteen years. Rode his first pipe about twelve years ago, a splintering fiberglass deathtrap at some prefabricated park in Arizona. Next up was a tipped-over concrete silo in an industrial wasteland in Dallas. Then last year he hit the Angie Pipe, a monstrous West Texas cathedral skated in the '70s and recently rediscovered and exploited by a crew led by *Thrasher* editor Jake Phelps. "We also got one going off in a secluded loca- tion west of Dallas," Cruzo taunts. "It's killer as shit. We've been trying to keep it low-key, but the word broke out. I know it wasn't any of our crew. Some peo- ple don't understand the concept of keeping some- thing low-key. They'd rather have people be impressed with their knowledge than, you know, having something around for a long time. I mean, you might score points with some guys, but there are guys who are gonna run around and run their mouth and tell everybody. And the next thing you know, it's gonna be a bust. We got a pretty tight crew—Ripper, Caleb, myself, and another guy—and we're all pretty tight. And with my stepson, we let him in on pools and he knows he'll get his ass whipped if he tells anyone. It's kind of selfish of us, but we've been burned too many times by these guys from other crews, and they're not . . . you gotta understand, these are the guys that will . . . I mean, I guess the best way I could describe them would be like leeches."

IF OBSESSIVE POOL SKATERS are a tight-lipped bunch, then true pipe skaters could be said to have their jaws wired shut. Usually. But not always. Even the most vociferous preachers of time-honored etiquette can sometimes fail in practice. Take, for example, the article "Go Epic or Go Home" in *Thrasher*'s June 2000 issue, tagged on the cover as "Texas Pipe Mission."

The story, penned by longtime pipe master Steve "Salba" Alba, opens captivatingly, unfolding like a sacred map to a lost treasure. A dried-up photo of some unidentifiable '70s crew skating a massive pipe had surfaced from *Thrasher* archives, and Phelps was obsessed with pinpointing the pipe's location, at last calling on Salba for help. Dispatching his scouts, Salba locked down the pipe's whereabouts, the gist of which is revealed in the article's reprinted private email correspondence between Salba and Dusto, his Texas reconnaissance contact. Though the emails hint at paths to the pipe, *Thrasher* editors, with good judgment, blacked out all references to the pipe's precise

location, as well as any clues, whether glaring or subtle, that could be fitted together to tug away the article's veil of secrecy. But the ten-page spread also quotes a newspaper article published five days after Phelps, Salba, Dusto, and six others were arrested as they exited the pipe after three hours of skating. Though all location references in the newspaper article were blacked out as well, the headline and reporter's byline were not. Any halfway curious skateboarder with a brain and access to the Internet could simply type the reporter's name and the headline into a search engine and, with a few more mouse clicks, print out the story, which, in its lead sentence, lists the name of the reservoir from which the pipe drains. But, as it turns out, such searches were unnecessary—readers merely had to flip to the story's last page, which all but glows with the pipe's GPS coordinates. That final page holds booking photos—mug shots of Phelps and *Thrasher* photo editor Luke Ogden—that list the county in which they were arrested. On top of that, there's a copy of their bail bondsman's business card, complete with city address. While any clever explorer could follow a single portion of the provided path to this, as the story puts it, Great Pyramid of skateboarding's Giza, together the clues draw a map, listing the state, county, city, and, finally—bull's-eye—the reservoir.

So much for etiquette.

Honorably, however, in what seems an admission of guilt, Phelps did include a sidebar entitled "10 Things Not to Do on a Pipe Mission" (including such no-brainers as bringing nine people, parking near no-parking signs, and staying for three hours). But Salba's text concludes like a cover-up of flagrant mistakes and reeks with self-aggrandizement, glorifying the arrest as "the biggest bust in the history of skateboarding" and "the stuff legends and lore are made of."

While Salba admits to carelessness caused by a case of "pipe jones," Phelps blames the bust on Dusto's "bunk recon."

"We let somebody else do recon for us," Phelps says, "and they were claiming that they skated it and were all, 'Yeah, yeah. It's on.' And we got down there and it was a bag. It was rough . . . dusty, and there was water in parts of it and bolts sticking up . . . and nobody'd been there for like twenty years and we got busted and it fuckin' sucked."

Dusto defends: "It's cuz they stayed down there too long taking pictures and shit. The whole thing is . . . I went to that pipe—like what?—three or four times before I took those dudes there, and, my crew, we'd be in and outta there in an hour, you know? But with those dudes, they're like, 'We flew all the way down from California for this, so we're gonna skate for a while.' Three hours? And something else was that somehow BMX bikers found out about it. There's a crew of BMX guys that find full pipes also. And they started riding [Angie] Pipe soon after we had found it and it had gotten pretty blown out. The week before they busted us, the cops busted [a large group] of BMX dudes riding that pipe. They didn't arrest them. They just let them go. But when they caught us in there, they're like, 'No, we're gonna hafta arrest ya cuz it's gettin' too outta control.' It was just like the worst luck, man."

ROB "SLOB" WEEDMAN, LOUISVILLE, KENTUCKY, SEPTEMBER 2002

PHOTO: CHARLIE MIDDLETON

THE ARMY CORPS OF ENGINEERS DID US RIGHT, STROKED US GOOD, AND GAVE US THE BEST PIECE OF CONCRETE ON THE FACE OF THE EARTH

CRAIG JOHNSON, TEXAS PRO

In the larger world of skateboarding, *Thrasher's* publicized slip-up seems paltry. In truth, as Phelps points out, only a handful of skateboarders possess the financial wherewithal and obsessive drive to make the pilgrimage to sacred Texan pipe country. But the article burned many of the Texas skaters nonetheless. Like disciples betrayed by their trusted masters, a few shook their heads in disbelief at the article's careless hubris. And when they snapped out of their astounded denial, they lashed out in Internet chat rooms, all but demanding Phelps's head. Everybody has since clammed up considerably to anybody inquiring about the whereabouts and status of known Texas pipes. Even with perfect reconnaissance, accessing pipes has become more risky since the terrorist strikes of September 11, 2001, after which most major American

dams—crucial producers of water and power for entire regions—were placed under close watch by militant security.

WHEN DAYBREAK FINALLY PIERCES through, it's nearly 7:30, leaving Dusto, Caleb, Cruzo, Ripper, and Slim just an hour—an hour-fifteen, tops—to ride before the lake's fixture fishermen and prowling rangers cut into

good-day/bad-day things, and I know next time I'm just going to have to make it good."

Ripper, now working up a sweat through four layers of clothing, is so captivated by the velocity and flow he can't feel the bitter cold against his face or hear the thunderous echo of howling urethane against cold concrete.

Dusto—no helmet, no pads—hits the highest lines of the morning, frontside rainbows well over vert, skating it like he's been here before, working the elbow's converging curves before arching toward the spillway and screaming through the darkness between the elbow and mouth, instinctively dodging a few rough spots and scatterings of dirt.

Caleb's found the flow, for sure, taking to the pipe

TEJAS IS A BUST
STEVE "SALBA" ALBA

their chances for an undetected exit. The riding begins with little warm-up; from the get-go, they all have at it with everything they've got. They take turns shoving off from the elbow and ride the glassy concrete in long, carving arches toward the pipe's mouth, climbing higher, higher, higher with each turn until they're beyond ninety degrees and diving back toward the opposite wall—like bombing a hill—at high speed.

Slim's soaring across acres of "skatepark-smooth" concrete, rushing in slow motion through the Promised Land. "That was a spiritual experience for me," he'd say later. "I mean, not to sound cheesy. But I'm thirty-seven years old and I've skated mass backyard pools, ditches, pretty much everything, but that was The Shit. That was It. You know what I mean? Fucking unreal."

Cruzo, more at ease with the tight lines of backyard pools, pads up and works on getting a feel for some of the biggest curves he's ever ridden. "But I don't have that nice thrusting flow that I should have," he realizes. "I just don't have the right pump. It's one of those

like a lifelong surfer to a tropical wave. "I've surfed huge waves," he would later relate, "and skating that pipe felt more like surfing to me than skating." But ten minutes into the session, he goes down, a daybreak body-slam hard against frozen concrete—one of the most unforgettably painful experiences in skateboarding—tumbling to a stop with warm red stuff dripping from his newly crushed right index finger. He gets up and keeps riding.

About an hour later, Dusto glances at his watch. Time to split. They draw their final lines, crack cold beers, kick back for a moment at the mouth, waves of steam levitating from warm bodies. But before packing up to retrace their approach path, gather the rope, and refasten the cyclone fence, each will leave behind just one sign of their trip of a lifetime. Ripper whips out a black felt-tip and signs his name to the wall, adding his notch to those of three decades before him. He passes on the Sharpie and each scrawls his name, but when it comes to Caleb, the pen's dry. Caleb shrugs, lifts his battered finger, and signs in blood.

6 THE '80s

SKATE & DESTROY

GAVIN O'BRIEN
HAS A THEORY.
HE CALLS IT
THE
SKATE-
BOARDER'S
ADVANTAGE:

IF A PERSON HAS LEARNED THE INTRICACIES OF BALANCE, CONFIDENCE, STYLE, AND CREATIVITY THAT ARE INHERENT TO SKATEBOARDING, THEN EVERYTHING ELSE COMES EASY.

Most skateboarders, he explains, excel at adapting. Urban cores crawl with skateboarders snapping down towering staircases, grinding around curving curbs, sliding smoothly away from steep handrails, and dodging deadly traffic. Suburban tracts are home to skateboarders who sneak over high fences and tall walls to scout out, clean out, and ride abandoned swimming pools. Rural realms coax ramp-hungry teenagers down dirt roads at midnight to poach plywood and two-by-fours from construction sites. And, O'Brien continues, as these skateboarders mature, chasing curiosity with an open mind, they adapt rapidly to most other pursuits. "I know guys that started riding motorcross, playing ice hockey, wakeboarding . . . their own businesses, you name it, and they have excelled faster than the average pedestrian status-quo jock." Same goes for playing an instrument or writing lyrics for a punk band. O'Brien sings.

Ray Stevens II plays bass. His axe is a 1979 Fender Jazz, and he sends it through a five-hundred-watt Peavey PA head, for that great-sounding bottom-end boom that's tough on amplifiers. Stevens blows out amps quite often. "For some reason I just hit them kinda hard," he shrugs. "I just throw thunderbolts." Stevens's thunderbolts crash from a dark storm that's been brightening the sky of punk rock for more than two decades. Inheriting an Electra bass and an ear for music from his grandfather, Stevens first started playing and reading music in sixth grade, the same time he started skateboarding. His junior high music teacher, Mr. Taylor, was "cool as fuck," Stevens remembers. "He skated and surfed and had pictures of Sid Vicious and John Coltrane on his walls and would tell us all music is good." With young Stevens on bass, Mr. Taylor taught his band the Commodores' "Brick House," and they played it in front of the school. By the time he was halfway through high school, punk rock had seduced Stevens, and he soon joined up with some older rockers to play Avengers, Victims, and

Tim Brauch

SAN JOSE

DEL'S WALL

PHOTO: CHRIS Kardas

STEVE CABALLERO – JAN. 1986
HIS RAMP   PHOTO: BRITTAIN

Dead Kennedys covers at summer parties. When he went back to school in the fall, the locker-room jocks heckled him for being a punker. When the tormenting football players jogged outside for practice, Stevens, living up to his new moniker, whipped it out in front of the mesh locker doors and pissed all over their clothes. After school, life was music and skateboarding, mostly in that order, and in 1981 he helped build Los Olvidados (The Forgotten), his first real band, a punk outfit that had a lot of musical influence on a young skateboarder named Steve Caballero.

Caballero is one of the world's greatest skateboarders. His trophy shelf may not be as big as Tony Hawk's, but he built it with better style. He skates smooth as ice, pumping through easy tricks like blood through a beating heart and taming tough tricks into pictures of perfection. Caballero dismisses O'Brien's theory. "I pick up other things quickly not so much because of my skateboarding, but more because of my attitude to succeed, my attitude of learning," he says. "I'm good at focusing on one thing until I get good at it. I don't believe in natural talent at all. People use the term *natural talent* very loosely and don't see the hard work somebody puts into something to be good at it." That said, Caballero could still very well represent the smoking gun, the most convincing piece of evidence backing O'Brien's theory. As a skateboarder, Caballero is an all-around ripper, running streets, tearing ramps, and burning bowls with equal and outstanding doses of abusive fluidity. So, theoretically, of course he's good at playing chess, riding motorcycles, designing skateboard shoes, racing radio-controlled cars, and learning music. Caballero plays guitar.

Keith Rendon plays drums. When he was thirteen, his uncle Dave loaned him a drum set and taught him how to tune and care for it. "I just picked it up," he remembers. "I knew I could play drums before I even started." He'd practice in the garage, keeping time with his favorite bands, namely the Clash and the Sex Pistols. His first record was a Dead Kennedys twelve-inch, *Fresh Fruit*. His mom bought it for him. When Rendon wasn't enthusiastically playing drums or reluctantly going to school, he was skateboarding. He used to take the bus alone to skate by himself at

SOME NIGHTS WE WERE PLAYING BASEMENTS, YOU KNOW, AND WE WERE JUST PLAYING WHATEVER, BACKYARD PARTIES, OR PLAYING ON THE FLAT BOTTOM OF SOME HALF-PIPE IN MIDLAND, TEXAS. SERIOUSLY. WE WOULD DRIVE ALL NIGHT FROM NEW MEXICO TO TEXAS TO PLAY SOME, YOU KNOW, SOME PARTY THAT GOT BUSTED DURING OUR SECOND SONG. ADAM WOULD BOOK WHATEVER HE COULD GET. IT'S HARSH, BUT THAT'S WHAT YOU'VE GOT TO DO. I KNOW THE FIRST TIME THEY TOURED, BEFORE I WAS IN THE BAND, WAS EVEN HARDER. YOU'D PLAY A SHITTY SHOW, A SHITTY SHOW, A SHITTY SHOW, THEN—BAM!—YOU'D PLAY A HUGE, OUT-OF-HAND, CRAZY, GREAT SHOW. OR ONE NIGHT YOU'RE PLAYING SOMEBODY'S BASEMENT IN CONNECTICUT, THEN THE NEXT NIGHT YOU'RE IN NEW YORK AT CBGB'S
RAY STEVENS

Winchester Skatepark, where the older skaters, including Gavin O'Brien, vibed him.

Together, O'Brien, Stevens, Caballero, and Rendon

THE EARLY '80S WERE REALLY, REALLY GOOD AND RAW. JUST SKATING AROUND, FINDING THE ROOTS IN THE STREET AGAIN; THE INDUSTRY WAS DOWN, THE SKATEPARKS DIED, THERE WAS NO MONEY BEING MADE. AND IF YOU WERE A REAL SKATER, YOU WERE GOING TO KEEP SKATING, BUT YOU WERE GOING TO ADAPT TO WHAT WAS GOING ON, RIGHT?

KEITH MEEK, FORMER PRO

and Caballero booted him from the band, replacing him with O'Brien, who was always singing along to whatever hardcore was blasting from his makeshift boom-box car stereo. As Eric departed, Craig ditched the band to hit skins for the Unaware. Adam Segal replaced Bosch on drums, and Russ Wright played guitar. Soon, Segal moved to second guitar, leaving a hole for drummer Rendon, who was recruited by Caballero after they met at a TSOL show at San Francisco's On Broadway. Their first practice together belted from the back bedroom of Caballero's mom's house on Halloween 1982, supplying a punk-rock soundtrack for the heated skate session unfolding outside on Caballero's ramp, a nine-foot-high, twelve-foot-wide half-pipe nailed together from two-by-fours and plywood.

Rehearsing a handful of songs and sessioning the ramp out back, this band without a name spent entire afternoons jamming and skating. Crushing chords fired them up to skate; heated sessions boiled over into their music. Out of this alchemy of aggressive creativity came literally all their songs, including the seminal "Skate & Destroy," a classic tune that would soon become the tattoo across skateboarding's underbelly.

"All we wanted to do was just do it," O'Brien remembers. "We didn't know if we would ever record anything or play any shows. We just wanted to make some music." And Caballero: "It wasn't like we started a band as musicians; we just all skated."

Within weeks of their first practice, local skateboarder and music promoter Craig Ramsay, then twenty-one, who launched and operated Faction Productions, approached O'Brien and Caballero to record a handful of songs for a cassette compilation entitled *Growing Pains*. Promoted by word of mouth, on flyers, and through photocopied skate 'zines as "an intense 60 min. deluge of San Jose's hard-driving

form the Faction, a punk rock band born and based in San Jose, California. Caballero planted the band's original seed, and, as is the case with most bands, the Faction's deepest roots tapped the lives of many people whose contributions quickly came and went.

On Stevens's advice, Caballero scanned the walls at Guitar Center and picked out a bass fitting his diminutive stature. Stevens taught him how to tune it, and Caballero promptly mastered a few chords and called on fellow skateboarders Craig Bosch and Pat Hauser to join him on drums and guitar, respectively. Bosch's brother Eric sang but had a tough time with it,

LOS GATOS, CALIFORNIA, JUNE 1982   BOB DENIKE, SUMMIT RAMP,
PHOTO: TIM PIUMARTA, COURTESY OF BOB DENIKE

underground," Ramsay's sampler would feature Grim Reality, the Bruces, Ribzy, Executioner, the Unaware, Los Olvidados, Whipping Boy, and that band of skaters who practiced and skated every day at Caballero's house. Problem was, that band didn't have a name. Depending on who's telling the story, O'Brien either hit up Ramsay for the use of his company name or Ramsay offered it. Either way, the Faction was born.

In late November 1982, the Faction booked their first gig. By O'Brien's estimate, San Jose's punk scene was only a few hundred strong, and the collective leather-and-thrift-store smell of it pervaded San Jose City College's Union Hall on the night of Friday, December 3. The lineup: the Faction, Living Abortions, the Unaware, Ribzy, Los Olvidados, and, in the prime of their widespread influence within and without Southern California's cradle of hardcore, Social Distortion. O'Brien's memory: "We were nervous as fuck." But apparently, O'Brien "really poured on the emotion" and was able to channel his uneasiness into a "visual" stage show, according to an upstart reporter's review of the show published on the back page of the *City College Times*. The article goes on: "The singer screamed, the bass player played one string and the guitarist was never in control of his sound. Regardless, their sound did take up space and got the crowd slammin'."

The slam pit was a churning mess of punkers and skaters: two similar breeds, to be sure, but not to be confused. "We were looked down on cuz we didn't have spikes and mohawks," O'Brien remembers, "looked down on cuz we skated and didn't shoot heroin." And Caballero: "We got a lot of shit back in the day because we weren't the hardcore, Oi!, leather-jacketed, spiked-hair-looking punks." And the resentment extended beyond the music venues. In fact, the stares could be much icier at home and on the streets. "I got

IT'S INCREDIBLE HOW SKATEBOARDING AND MUSIC AFFECTED ALL OF OUR LIVES. THIS WHOLE SAN JOSE SCENE. IT WAS LIKE, "OH, THIS IS AN AMAZING THING THAT WE HAVE AND WE DON'T KNOW WHERE IT'S GOING, BUT FOR RIGHT NOW, TODAY 'FUCK YEAH!'"

MARK WATERS, SAN JOSE–BRED SKATER

kicked out at seventeen for cutting my hair too short," O'Brien says. "And back then, if you were walking down the street and had Vans on and straight-leg jeans and short hair that was maybe dyed, random people would get out of their cars and kick your ass. That was daily life for me back then." O'Brien's younger brother, Corey, who skated professionally for Santa Cruz Skateboards during the late '80s and early '90s, adds: "If you had short hair back then, anything above the ear, you were a freak. Everybody had feathered hair back then, and long hair. And we wore Levis that weren't flared out at the bottom. You were a freak if you wore that with some Converse and an Indy shirt or something. You were just a freak." Hunted in the streets, the O'Brien brothers and the rest of the skaters and punkers found solidarity in a subscene woven from the threads of skateboarding and music.

Within a year of recording *Growing Pains*, Russ Wright had left the band, and the Faction played as a four-piece until '84, around the same time that Stevens's Los Olvidados broke up. Drawn by the synchronized blast of two guitars, Caballero dropped his four-string for a six-string and asked Stevens to join the band on bass. Stevens respected the Faction's drive, not only on stage but in the studio and on the road. "When the Faction asked me to join, I was like, 'Hey, can we put out records?' and they were like, 'Yeah.' And I'm all, 'Can we tour?' 'Yeah.' And I was all, 'Okay, I'm in,'" he remembers. "It was definitely something I was ready to do."

Plenty of other bands at the time accused the Faction of riding Caballero's coat-tails. It didn't hurt, of course, that a top professional skateboarder was in the band. But behind Caballero's motivation and underground celebrity was a band of young men—also skateboarders—who wasted little time waiting around to be discovered. The Faction got off their asses and practiced. A lot. Often five days a week. In two and a half years they wrote thirty-four songs and recorded one tape, one LP, and four EPs; they were also featured on several compilations, including the first two volumes of *Thrasher's Skate Rock*. They took any show

that came their way or along the way, playing a damp basement one night and a big-city hall the next. Caballero, too, always pushed merchandise, printing homemade stickers and T-shirts and selling them on the road to pay for gas and food. Together they represented what a band could be: a group of driven musicians with deep, common roots, who played music—music they liked to listen (and skate) to—for themselves and often for a strong throng of like-minded fans.

So, naturally, it didn't last. After one final gig, the Faction broke up on Halloween 1985, three years to the day from their first real jam session in the back bedroom of Caballero's mom's house. The Faction, like many bands, broke up because they disagreed on the direction the music was taking. Four years later, they reunited for a benefit gig for a murdered musician friend, and then a year later they played a pair of sold-out reunion shows, with Indiana-bred ex–pro skateboarder Jeff Kendall filling in for Segal on guitar. Then nothing for more than a decade, mainly because O'Brien was half nervous, half uninterested in getting back up on stage to sing songs he'd written two decades back. "We were early-'80s skate rock," O'Brien told *Juice* magazine in 2002. "And that's great. I wouldn't have traded that for anything, but the reason I finally caved is that Mike Fox [a highly respected guitarist for Los Olvidados, Hemi, and the Dwarves, among others] called me up one night and bawled me out for about an hour. Three days later, I called Stevie [Caballero] and said, 'All right, let's do it.'" The Faction was back.

ON A CLEAR SUMMER FRIDAY AFTERNOON in 1981, less than a month after Winchester Skatepark had closed forever, Craig Ramsay, Ross McGowan, and Bob Denike piled inside a small Cessna passenger plane piloted by Ramsay's younger sister, Maureen, and lifted off the tarmac at

San Jose Airport. Soaring low over the middle of town, Maureen, still in high school at the time, dipped a wing, giving her passengers a better look at the urban spread below. That's when they spotted it—a half-empty swimming pool tucked behind an apartment complex. Maureen circled. With a pushpin, Ramsay marked the pool's position on a street map. "Okay, got

it," he told his sister. Maureen banked toward the next neighborhood, and they continued their search.

Following their map the next morning, Ramsay, Denike, and McGowan pulled up to a beat-down apartment complex on San Tomas Aquino Road and peeked over its fence. There she was. A huge swimming pool shaped sort of like a squared-off boomerang. The three hungry skateboarders walked through the gate and stood at the pool's lip. She was a mess, a jagged pool of slime, a putrid pond of stagnant water and rusted junk. A busted refrigerator and a dented stove stuck from the muck.

As they considered the cleanup and looked at one another, trying to decide if the pit was worth the work, the property manager burst from his upstairs apartment. Built like a fire hydrant, covered with tats, and crowned with a flattop, the ex-Marine glared down at the three scrawny skaters through mirrored sunglasses. "What the hell do you guys want?" he yelled.

McGowan and Denike bolted for the gate. But Ramsay stayed put. "We're looking for pools to ride our skateboards in," he replied, which served only to further irritate the former killing machine, as if the word *skateboards* had actually been a porcupine shoved up his ass.

"If you're not off the property in ten seconds, I'm getting my gun!" he screamed.

Though threatened and outgunned, Ramsay stood his ground. Instead of running, he reasoned, explaining that he had been an employee in good standing at Winchester Skatepark, that he and his friends were professional-level skateboarders, and that they were willing to clean out the pool in exchange for permission to ride. Besides, the stinking pit was obviously a health hazard, and if some child fell in and died, somebody would be held liable, most likely the property manager.

A small light sparked behind the mirrored sunglasses. "Okay, you've got the rest of the weekend to get it cleaned out," he told the skateboarders, "and I might have some more work around here for you to do before I let you skate in there."

The skaters nodded their heads and smiled at one another. "We had a debate right then," remembers Ramsay, "thinking, 'If we got five more guys, we'd be skating that same day.' But we were all of the same mind: let's keep it between us. Our constant fear was overexposure of our pools."

As long shadows obscured the pool's smooth curves, Ramsay, Denike, and McGowan scooped the final buckets of blackwater and last soggy heaps of trash from the deep end. It had taken their combined strength to muscle the stove and fridge up the shallow-end steps. "We worked from 10 A.M. till dark and hosed it down that night," remembers Ramsay. "We couldn't really see how good it was, and when we came back the next morning, we came around the corner and saw it. We're all, 'This thing's so hot!' and just started ripping it. We didn't even check in with the Drill Sergeant. We figured we'd get some runs in before he changed his mind."

During that inaugural session, they dubbed the pool STAR, an acronym for San Tomas Aquino Road, and vowed to keep it covert for as long as possible, which ended up being about two months, a respectable span of secrecy considering the strong temptation to share with others this hole in the ground, overflowing with long afternoons of cold beer and heated sessions. To keep STAR alive, they regularly checked in with the Drill Sergeant, who'd have them pruning shrubs, making dump runs, even tiling a bathroom in exchange for private sessions on perfect trannies.

As the crown jewel of their collection, the STAR Pool was never offered as a "bowl for barter" under the auspices of the San Jose Pool Exchange, their backyard terrain cooperative, launched that same summer. On the wing and on the road, the Pool Exchange founding fathers were constantly prowling for abandoned bowls. Denike also worked that summer as a draftsman for the city of Campbell, rendering technical drawings of street intersections and double-checking his renditions against aerial photographs, some of

WE WENT TO A RECORD STORE HERE IN SAN JOSE AND SAW THAT FIRST JFA SINGLE HANGING ON THE WALL, WITH THOSE GUYS ON THE COVER RIDING DUANE PETERS BOARDS, AND WE WERE BLOWN AWAY. AND THEY WERE SINGING ABOUT COKES AND SNICKERS AND STUFF WE COULD TOTALLY RELATE TO

COREY O'BRIEN

which showed entire neighborhoods dotted with swimming pools. He took note. Once located and cleaned, a pool was logged onto a status sheet that listed the pool's name, the date found, its location, the names of the finders/informants, those authorized by SJPE to skate it, skaters with privileges pending, and when the pool was open for riding. By fall, the backyard bounty proved to be more pools than they could skate in an entire weekend, dozens of bowls in a detailed compendium always under Ramsay's close watch. "Eventually other skaters caught on to our pools and would be begging us to take them, but we didn't want to blow them out, so we kept it tight," Ramsay recalls. "And if you wanted us to take you to one of our pools, you had to provide us with a pool of equal or better value. We also had a short list of sacred pools so pristine that there was no way we'd ever take you there. STAR was one of them."

"Yeah, the San Jose Pool Exchange were the older guys—Ramsay, Denike," says Gavin O'Brien, laughing. "They kind of burned us. We took them to a sick pool once and they gave us some shitty ditch." Denike remembers that one: "We were kinda assholes about it, actually. I hate to say that. We'd exchange some pretty shitty pools for good ones. Tempting them with, 'We'll give you two pools for one.' Two really shitty ones. Back then, you know, Corey and Gavin were a bit younger than us, and we took advantage of that."

ON JULY 31, 1981, a couple hundred skateboarders filled Winchester Skatepark, throwing down their last rides on the park's last day. More than three years earlier, the *San Jose Mercury News* had announced that skateboard parks were destined for permanence, representing expensive, concrete proof of skateboarding's staying power. But as the industry waned during the late '70s, skateparks closed down like bars during Prohibition. Some blamed the decline on an industry that ate its own; some say the wider "pig" boards became so popular so fast that the overstock of skinnier mid-'70s models sat unsold, undermining business; and some say it just got lame, too popular and blown out, and many original skateboarders returned to the underground. On Saturday morning, August 1, the front page of the *Mercury*'s "Living" section featured an edge-to-edge, above-the-fold photograph of Caballero on the last day at his home park, blasting a frontside air from the deep-end wave of concrete swelling from a gigantic washboard. What surprised many of San Jose's core skaters was not that a mainstream news outlet had actually, for once, published a decent, if not exceptional, skateboarding photo—what made them smirk and shake their heads was the headline: "The Twilight of the Skateboard."

Like predicting the demise of snowboarding with widespread resort closures, like expecting band breakups as venues shut down, the paper had erroneously hitched the whole of skateboarding to the rapidly sinking ship of pay-to-skate parks. Even before the parks closed, San Jose had simmered with thriving underground scenes, one of which unfolded slowly on the edge of a strip mall parking lot in South San Jose, on the corner of Pearl and Branum.

"The Scurbs [short for skateable curbs] were kinda by my house when I lived with my mom still," Corey O'Brien remembers. "We'd go get Cokes and just hang out. We didn't have money to go to Winchester, so we'd just hang out in the parking lot, and we skated cuz we were just bored sitting there, and we'd do our skatepark tricks on the curbs. At first it was just a hangout. We'd be sitting on our boards and then we'd push off and drop off the platform and hit the other curb and try to do a one- or two-foot slide or something, stupid backside tail slides, you know, doing vert tricks on the curb. Sweepers. Layback roll-outs. Just weird shit. It wasn't that big of a deal, but it was where we started street skating." The year was 1980.

By that time, the industry was all but belly up, skateparks were an endangered species, and the O'Brien brothers and the rest were regularly getting hassled for running Converse, jeans, flannels, and dyed hair. It was a tough time to be a skateboarder, but, as many will relate, it was a golden era as well. First off, skateboarding had found its soundtrack, music served raw in bare-bones venues capped with naked rafters and floored with booze-stained concrete, filled with working-stiff male camaraderie, chicks in spikes and nets, sloppy fights, and blue-collar bands. Also, the skate scene thinned out—weekend park skaters, now with no place to ride, closeted their sticks and went back to baseball and BMX—leaving emphatic evidence of who was in it for the long haul and who wasn't. The scene wasn't much, but it belonged to the skaters, who again bolstered it by building driveway quarterpipes and backyard half-pipes, prowling for pools, and taking their talents and boredom to the surrounding, growing urban Babylon. This movement back to the parking lots and sidewalks—and it didn't happen only

ONE LAST THING I'LL SAY ABOUT SKATEBOARDING AND SAN JOSE AND EVERYTHING . . . IT WAS LIKE, YOU JUST DID IT. IT'S HARD TO THINK BACK ABOUT IT. CUZ WHEN YOU LOOK BACK AT ALL THE STUFF WE DID, IT'S KINDA AMAZING, THE RAMPS AND THE POOLS, BUT, YOU KNOW, WE DIDN'T KNOW ANY BETTER. YOU KNOW WHAT I MEAN? THE ENERGY WE HAD BACK THEN WAS JUST AMAZING, AS SKATEBOARDERS, AS MUSICIANS; A LOT OF GUYS WERE ARTISTS. THAT'S WHAT'S GREAT ABOUT SKATEBOARDERS: THEY'RE SO MULTIFACETED. YOU DID A LOT OF CREATIVE STUFF, BUT AT THE TIME YOU DIDN'T KNOW IT, YOU'RE JUST SO CLOSE TO THE FIRE
BOB DENIKE

in San Jose—marked a quiet resurrection of the original street seed from which skateboarding had first grown.

"Even while the parks were in full swing, there was a hardcore contingent of skaters in San Jose who were out riding the streets and building ramps," Ramsay recalls. "The scene was strong even without the parks and industry support. When the parks went, I think that the core skaters just got a lot more serious about staying in touch, hitting the local spots, and finding ways to keep the scene alive." Even *before* the parks had opened, Ramsay adds, San Jose had a strong scene, with skateboarders such as the Buck brothers, Peter "Kiwi" Gifford, the Thatcher brothers (Kevin Thatcher would launch and edit *Thrasher* in 1981), Rick Blackhart (Northern California's answer to Tony Alva), and others pushing limits at Los Altos Pool, Bombora Pipe, Uvas spillway, and other spots.

Down at the Scurbs, the O'Brien brothers and a few others were, out of boredom mostly, perfecting their slides and grinds, often sessioning for hours on end until hunger called, fatigue set in, or the cops rolled up. (After blowing off a few warnings, Corey, then fourteen, was arrested for skateboarding in the Scurbs

parking lot and hauled downtown, where his mom had to fetch him. It was the beginning of a long hate-hate relationship between Corey and the cops.) In 1981, the Scurbs locals took a quick trip down south to skate the few survivors of what some call the Skatepark Genocide. In the parking lot of Whittier skatepark, Gavin showed Southland ripper John Lucero—who now runs Black Label Skateboards out of Costa Mesa—a frontside 50-50 (a double-truck grind, facing the lip). "I did a 50-50 and Lucero freaked out and learned them and a few months later got the sequence in *Thrasher* and called it a slappy and got all the credit. I invented slappies, but I never called them that. I called them 50-50s, after the same trick on vert. I admit I was pretty jealous he got the credit." (Lucero rebuts: "Gavin didn't show me the slappy—I've been skating curbs like that since 1977 or 1978. But if he wants the credit, he can have it.")

A decade later, a new generation—tapping skateable terrain on every street corner in America and beyond—would warm up with a few curb boardslides and 50-50s before taking this "street style" to the next level, to steep handrails and waist-high marble planter boxes. And in doing so they would redirect the entire industry with a few maneuvers that were once simple, yet creative, cures for common teenage boredom.

IT'S APRIL 19, 2003. Corey O'Brien's Blank Club is a dark, roomy, nondescript box of a music venue just off the main drag in downtown San Jose. Bulbs ringing the room halfway between the slab floor and high ceiling provide a blood-red ambiance. A handful of Naugahyde booths runs down one wall; a horseshoe booth caps one end of the L-shaped bar. Over wells and shelves of booze and thirteen beers on tap, a large sign shines "Pabst Blue Ribbon." The men's room is wallpapered with old flyers from early-'80s hardcore shows. Adolescents. Black Flag. Channel 3. China White. Jodie Foster's Army. Mentors. Misfits. Los Olvidados. Samhain. And, of course, the Faction.

PUNK AND SKATEBOARDING WENT TOGETHER CUZ THEY SHARED RAW ENERGY. NOT SO PRECISE. JUST GOING WITH THE FLOW. IMPROVISED. THE WAY IT DROVE YOU AND MADE YOU FEEL
STEVE CABALLERO

By 10:30 P.M. the Blank Club is nearing capacity: Some two hundred heads are drinking and chatting inside, and another two dozen are outside smoking. The evening's opening band, the Shit Kickers, steps to the corner stage and lays into a set, carried by a strumming banjo player, a bearded man on fiddle, an acoustic guitarist, a left-handed bassist, a smoking drummer girl, and a mustached singer in a mesh camouflage hat. Fans dance like mountain men on moonshine. Within forty minutes the Shit Kickers wrap it up to applause and a few yee-haws.

Steve Caballero leaves his post near the front door, where he's been selling T-shirts and stickers for the past ninety minutes, to fetch his Fender Strat. Ray Stevens, sporting a red shirt that says "Twenty Year Skateboarder," tunes his bass. Keith Rendon, wearing a black wife-beater and red surf trunks, surrounds himself with drums and cymbals. Gavin O'Brien loosens his vocal cords with black stout. And they're off . . . laying into an instrumental intro that grinds like a stripped-down, metal-edged Dick Dale surf riff. As it dissolves, O'Brien steps up to the mike, thanks the crowd for coming out, and dives into an old favorite: "Tongue Like a Battering Ram." The crowd sways, yells, sings along, hoists beers and cocktails, and O'Brien's all over the stage, snapping his mike cord like a whip and singing, "She's gotta tongue like a battering ram; someone oughta put her in her place!" At song's end, the crowd's hooting, a bunch of old friends seeing a band they've been listening to for twenty years.

"Can I get three pints of Guinness up here?" Gavin, thirty-eight, calls to the bar. "One for me, one for me, and one for me." As they blaze through "Lost in Space," the sweat's starting to show through Gavin's Devo "Are we not men?" shirt, and Stevens, thirty-nine, Caballero, thirty-eight, and Rendon, thirty-four, are cheating years from their biological ages, pouring it on like overamped teenagers set free with limitless wattage. A hole opens in the center of the crowd as a few shirtless guys put the first spins on the slam pit.

Eighties pro-turned-skateboard-shoe-mogul Tony Magnussen is spotted at the bar. Dave Hackett, a '70s champion still at it, watches from near the sound booth. Steve Olson, 1978 Skateboarder of the Year, is chatting up a few gals half his age. The Oregon-born park builder and president of Dreamland Skateparks, Mark "Red" Scott, in town to meet with San Jose city officials, has drained a few Pabst pints and winds up on stage as Caballero calls to the crowd, "Did you know that San Jose is finally gonna build a skatepark?"

"Dreamland style," Ray adds.

"And it only took twenty-five fucking years," yells Caballero before Ray bashes into the first rumbling notes of "Skate & Destroy."

With that, Red gives the gig its first stage dive.

Gavin belts out the anthem:

FORGET THE LIGHT, SKATE AND DESTROY
PASS THE JOGGER, SKATE AND DESTROY
SNAP IT BACK, SKATE AND DESTROY
KICK THAT BIKE, SKATE AND DESTROY

IT'S NOT A CAUSE OR POLITICAL BELIEF, IT'S SOMETHING
    IN MY THINKING
IF YOU AGREE IT'S COOL BY ME, AT LEAST I'M NOT A ROBOT
I'M NOT AFRAID OF THINGS I READ, I WON'T DIVIDE MY
    FRIENDS UP
DICTATORSHIP OF PEOPLE'S MINDS IS NOT WHAT I
    WILL STRIVE FOR

THE COPS ARE COMING AFTER ME, THEIR SONS ARE BMXERS
THEY ALWAYS TRY TO STOP ME BUT URETHANE IS FASTER
    THAN BOOTS
YOU MAY BE IN A PARKING LOT THROWING UP YOUR CONTENTS
SO WHAT WHO CARES I KNOW I DON'T
BE A HOOD, DON'T BE GOOD.

7

RAMPS

(CHRIST)

SWEATING WITH FEARFUL HUMILITY

AS IF STANDING BEFORE HIS GOD, CHRISTIAN HOSOI TREMBLED AS HE SPOKE. "MY LORD," HE STARTED, THEN CORRECTED HIMSELF.

"Your Honor . . . My purpose is to serve Jesus Christ and to speak out against drugs and what they do to our children. . . . I have a purpose-driven life now. . . . I am a new man."

With the final words of Hosoi's spiritual redemption, as friends and family bore witness to this thirty-five-year-old, ex–professional skateboarder at a crossroads with freedom, Judge Alan C. Kay's fourth-floor courtroom in downtown Honolulu became as somber and quiet as a church. Much more than a process of justice, the afternoon unfolded as a test of Hosoi's faith. And only the penitent man would pass.

During the previous hour, as the hopeful born-again had sat quietly in a blue-collared prison pullover, dark hair short and slick, his lawyer, Myles S. Breiner, had turned a foreboding day in court to Hosoi's favor. Hosoi originally had been sentenced to seventy months, but the law had since changed, enabling federal prosecutors the opportunity to drag Hosoi back

before the judge for a potentially stiffer sentence. But with the aggressive and respectful aim of a man who thinks sharply and quickly on his feet, Breiner categorically fended off, rebuked, and shot down a series of prosecutorial arguments poised to prolong Hosoi's prison stint. On top of that, Breiner emphasized that Hosoi had excelled personally and spiritually during his forty-two months behind bars—the dropout earned his high school diploma; the skateboard legend wrote inspirational letters to admiring upstarts; the new Christian conducted Bible studies; the hard worker volunteered regularly and never caused any trouble. In all respects, Breiner argued, the Hosoi before Judge Kay that afternoon—Friday, July 11, 2003—was the golden antithesis of the washed-up, strung-out, drug-running mule dangling by the end of his rope whom federal agents had arrested on Wednesday, January 26, 2000, in Honolulu's international airport with six hundred grams of crystal methamphetamine in his hip bag.

From the get-go, Judge Kay, who's also a religious man, had seemed driven by the sympathy he had

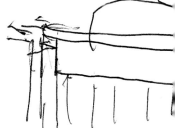

7.11.03

D.A. FIOCTA

PREVIOUS:
CHRISTIAN ROSHA HOSOI'S RESENTENCING,
JUDGE ALAN C. KAY'S COURTROOM, HONOLULU,
HAWAII, JULY 11, 2003
TRIPTYCH BY IVAN "POPS" HOSOI
LEFT:
CHRISTIAN HOSOI, ECHO PARK, CALIFORNIA, CIRCA 1990
PHOTO: IVAN "POPS" HOSOI

gathered from more than one hundred letters sent to his chambers by skateboarders, community leaders, and corrections officers lauding Hosoi's positive influence as a role model. When prosecutors moved to postpone the proceedings in order to investigate how Breiner had managed to erase a handful of Hosoi's prior convictions, Kay moved forward with the sentencing "to accommodate the family that is gathered here," he said. Behind Hosoi sat his wife, his mother and father, an uncle, a handful of cousins, and a dozen friends, mostly skateboarders, among them Hawaiian deejay Grant Fukuda, artist Jef Hartsel, and mainland legend Steve "Salba" Alba, who happened to be on the island vacationing with his family.

Judge Kay's sympathy, however, also spread to the

feds: he granted them one week to investigate the integrity of the orders that had erased Hosoi's priors. If the feds failed to find flaw, Kay's new sentence for Hosoi would stand.

Courtroom tension thickened. Hosoi's wife, Jennifer, blonde hair piled up away from tear-streaked cheeks, swallowed her sobs. She knew the feds were gunning for more time. But she also knew that Breiner had counterpunched solidly when he had convinced the court that, actually, her husband should receive a lesser sentence. Breiner explained that Hosoi's crime had not involved firearms or violence or resulted in loss of life; he had not supervised the drug-running outfit he was trafficking for; he had accepted responsibility for his lawbreaking and voluntarily checked into rehab; and last—and, in this case, most important—Hosoi no longer shouldered the legal burden of his priors.

Jennifer, however, remained on pins and needles. Yes, she remembered Judge Kay's compassion on June 19, 2001, when, moments after sentencing, he had married Christian and Jennifer right there in that same courtroom. But she also knew Judge Kay was a man bound by law to put away drug runners. Family and friends reassured her, but comforting words could not convince her of her man's imminent freedom. She would believe it only when they were walking hand in hand again, beneath the open sky.

Jennifer cried some more as prosecutors had their final say. U.S. attorney Chris Thomas pointed out that during Hosoi's early days of incarceration, at the Central Detention Center in San Bernardino,

California, the uncooperative drug addict—fearing the deadly consequences of wearing a rat jacket in prison—had sent DEA agents on a wild goose chase when asked to pinpoint the cartel's kingpins, people who still may be selling drugs today. In conclusion, Thomas submitted that Judge Kay should not let Hosoi off easy.

Hosoi stood to receive his sentence, chin up, as prepared as possible to meet his fate.

"I trust that with your new view on life you'll be able to conquer that addiction," Judge Kay said before handing down the most lenient sentence possible under his discretion. Forty-one months. Counting time served, Hosoi, at that moment, essentially became a free man. But he'd have to wait a week, praying all the while that prosecutors would not wedge another wrench into the slow-turning wheels of justice.

"You have been thoroughly tested and challenged," Judge Kay told Hosoi. "And I expect you to fulfill your following. Can you promise me that?"

"I promise."

The gavel fell. Court adjourned. Hosoi turned to thank his friends and family. "God bless you guys," he called over his shoulder as guards escorted him back to Honolulu's Federal Detention Center. Friends and family filed from the courtroom and gathered outside, emotions and hopes mixed and blown around by the trade winds.

THE WORST THINGS THAT CAN HAPPEN to a man happen in prison, Hosoi says. "It's the bottom of the lowest point in anybody's life. The only thing worse than prison is death." Coming from Hosoi, a man who will always be widely recognized as one of the greatest skateboarders of all time, tales of bottoming out have a particular sting because his plunge from the top was such a long one.

Hosoi's physical genius and rock-star extravagance soared most impressively during the late '80s and early '90s. From prize money and sponsors, he pulled down

WHEN I FIRST SAW HIM SKATE MARINA, I HAD TO LOOK AWAY. IT WAS SCARY. HE WAS JUST FLYING OUT OF THE POOLS. BUT HE WAS ALWAYS IN CONTROL
BONNIE MITCHELL

roughly a quarter million each year, burning it as fast as he could rake it in. Friends called him Big Daddy because he always picked up the tab. Driving 5.0s and Harleys, he luxuriated in a $2,300-a-month hilltop estate, once home to W.C. Fields, off Sunset Boulevard. Lapping the planet regularly, he dominated demonstrations with his superior style and crowd-pleasing charisma. Battling at every contest, he gave the world's best tough runs for top trophy, typically trading first-place finishes with Tony Hawk.

This good life, however, began to crumble as an economic recession seized the nation and the popularity of vert skating—that big-ramp genre now a spectacle at most so-called extreme sports events—sank beneath the rising wave of street skating. A new generation of skateboarders, aided and abetted by nearly exclusive coverage in the mags, pulled its energy away from isolated vert contests and sent it back to the streets where skateboarding was born. Many of the day's top professional ramp riders fell out, unable to keep up with new techniques. Consequently, board sales dropped for vert skaters as the street urchins opted for smaller decks, smaller wheels, and narrower trucks, set-ups lighter and more responsive to their trick bag than the wider, heavier, high-speed planks suited for ramp riding. The magazines pounded the

IF WE TOLD THE TRUTH AS TO WHY CHRISTIAN LEFT THE COMPANIES HE DID, IT WOULD BE DEGRADING THE COMPANIES' BUSINESS AND MORAL ETHICS, AND WE DON'T WANT THAT IN PRINT. IF I HAD MY DRUTHERS, I'D SLAM THEM ALL, BUT CHRISTIAN ISN'T THAT KIND OF GUY. HE'S WALKING THE STEPS OF JESUS, AND JESUS FORGIVES

IVAN "POPS" HOSOI

final nails into the coffin, declaring, in so many words, "Vert is dead."

None of that, however, dissuaded Hosoi from skateboarding. Sure, board sales dropped, sponsors went belly up, and the kids became more stoked on learning how to frontside boardslide a handrail than on smacking an alley-oop body jar on an extension with four feet of vert. But Hosoi kept at it, always an outstanding all-around skateboarder, taking his name and ideas to a handful of companies that, to varying degrees, thrived and dived. By the mid-'90s he was between companies, living with his mother, and racking his brain for his next gig.

One morning he got up early to drop his mom at work, then, as was his tradition, found a chair at Big

and Tall bookstore off Melrose to drink coffee, to read, and to see and be seen. Suddenly, it hit him. "Focus." Focus Skateboards Unlimited. FSU. Otherwise known as Fuck Shit Up. It was the perfect name for his next venture, which he launched with silkscreen-keen Barrett "Chicken" Deck and two former pro skateboarders and friends from way back, Dave Duncan and Eddie Reategui.

"And it's like '95 now," Hosoi remembers, "and I'm running this business, Duncan's doing the investing, and Eddie's running the warehouse. And they're going, 'Christian, we're having a tough time selling these boards.' And I'm all, 'You just gotta call and drop my name and we'll get them sold. Ram it down their throats. Just tell them it's Christian Hosoi's company.' I had a reputation with every single skate shop in the world. Then we're selling like thirty grand a month, and for no advertisement at that time, that's like unheard of. Now we're making pants, jackets, and all these things. Now we're sponsoring snowboard guys. Now the Orange County scene's blowing up, disco-party-like, Disco 2000, and they're cruising to the clubs and it was a huge scene and they wanted to go out every night and drink and party, and that was a part of what promoting is. You gotta be at the places. And I'm a pro rider. I'm the advertiser, I'm the promoter, doing the clubs, doing that—what do they call that in business?—the *schmoozing* with all the representatives and professional riders and all the industry, and I'm getting out there, and of course they want to be out there, too. But tomorrow's work, and it's like three in the morning and I'm like, 'You guys gotta get home and get some sleep.' But see, how do you tell somebody that when you're doing it and you're part of the company? It wasn't in sync. It wasn't like here's the motor, here's the tires, here's the chassis, this is what it takes for a car to go, and somebody's gotta drive. So

CHRISTIAN HOSOI LOFTING A METHOD AIR, SEATTLE, WINTER 1989
PHOTO: STEVE KEENAN

LEFT:
CHRISTIAN HOSOI, BARRANCA RAMP, VENTURA, CALIFORNIA, 1984
PHOTO: SCOTT STARR

RIGHT:
CHRISTIAN HOSOI SPINNING A 540, DEL MAR SKATE RANCH, 1984
PHOTO: IVAN "POPS" HOSOI

it was just not working, and the company took a dive. I mean, I could get into the technicalities, but everybody went their own ways. And that's when meth came into my life."

Hosoi snorted meth for a few years before smoking it. At first, he remembers, it didn't seem to drag him down too much. He'd been smoking pot for much of his life, and getting high and skateboarding had always just flowed together. But at that point, instead of burning herb and skateboarding, he'd smoke meth first. And initially, he still performed at his usual world-class level. But eventually, he figures, the meth began to eat away at his twenty-five years of dedication. Smoking meth became more important than skateboarding, cutting into his traditions of practicing and sessioning on a daily basis, training for contests, focusing easily and with tremendous happiness on exactly what he had always loved doing.

Other things, too, mounted the pressure: his business had gone belly up; he'd been busted for smalltime drug offenses but had failed to take care of them. And his girlfriend gave birth to their baby boy, Christian Rhythm Hosoi, on July 23, 1997, but their relationship crumbled; and his future as a pro skateboarder looked dim.

"And with Christian and his ego," says Reategui, "there's no way he'd skate if he was going to skate bad. When you don't rip and you're the best in the world, people get bummed. So he stayed away from skating in front of people. It was a tough thing. Christian couldn't go out like that, skating bad in front of people. So he just didn't skate. He'd get a little high, and the next day, when he's supposed to skate, he'd be partied out, and it got to the point where he'd be all, 'I'll just skate tomorrow, tomorrow, tomorrow. I'll party today.'"

"[Drug] dependency . . . will numb you to the truth and the reality of your situation," Hosoi recalls. "All of a sudden the things that you cared about and the activities that you thought were primary in your life are now secondary. You're numb to the fact that drugs aren't good for you. . . . [Jennifer and I] met doing drugs a little bit. But she quit, [and she went] to

CHRISTIAN HOSOI, LIEN AIR, MARINA DEL REY SKATEPARK, CALIFORNIA, 1981
PHOTO COURTESY OF IVAN "POPS" HOSOI

tomorrow, tomorrow,' to the point where God said, 'You know what? Watch this, Christian. I'm gonna really open your eyes to the love I have for you. And it's not going to be easy. It's gonna be the hardest thing.'

"And it took a little while to get through it. But through it, me and my wife have grown spiritually. We had to make all these decisions that every inmate has to make—Are we going to stay together? And she's like, 'I'm here and I love you.' And I'm looking at so much time, and it was a bit of a catastrophe for a while, but then all I did was plant myself into the Word of God and trusted in God that everything was gonna work out."

A CHILD OF THE FIRST generation of skateparks, Hosoi cradled his talent in concrete. But it was on wooden ramps that he made his highest marks and pulled his most prominent fame.

After the skateparks of the '70s had suffered and ultimately closed under liability burdens, skateboarders of the early '80s created their own outlets to satisfy the vertical urge. Some took vert tricks to the streets, dorking laybacks on parking-lot curbs, unknowingly rebuilding an entire genre. Others revisited the swimming pools once coveted in the '70s, but for many skaters (especially in cooler climes), backyard bowls were few and far between. It didn't take much, however, for skateboarders to build their own vert. They begged, borrowed, heisted, and sometimes even purchased the stacks of plywood and two-by-fours needed to pound together a quarter-pipe ramp or, better yet, a towering half-pipe.

Ramp designs improved dramatically as skateboarders-turned-carpenters innovated building techniques and experimented with differently sized transitions and lips. Though a few cities and YMCAs opened decently funded "ramp parks," most of the

church. She wanted to be a Christian. And I was in love with her, but I couldn't kick drugs. She's like, 'I'm going to church and I quit drugs. I don't wanna do that anymore.' And I was like, 'All right.' And I went to church with her [for] the first time in my life. And I was like, 'Yeah, I need to quit and make a big comeback. I gotta stop this stuff.' But Satan and his persuasion . . . [And I'd say,] 'All right, I'll quit tomorrow, best structures remained hidden away in skaters' backyards.

"Me and Tony Hawk didn't stop skating when all the parks closed," says Hosoi. "Caballero and all of us, we went and skated backyard ramp contests for no money. *We skated contests for no money*. We weren't there for the money; we were there for the sheer enjoyment of doing something you love to do. The ramps came in at that time because everyone needed them. They were a necessity. You didn't have anywhere to skate if you were a vert rider. And that's why street skating slowly crept in at the time, too.

"Yeah, skateboarding kinda had a lull, to the public. But to the pros it was thriving. We were searching out spots, going to Europe, doing full tours over there. Skateboarding was to the public a little underground, but to us it was our lifestyle. It wasn't a business. It wasn't something we did in the off-season. It wasn't something we did cuz it was publicized or cuz the media was on it.

"[In the '70s,] there was the full banners and all the cameras and staff members, and they made this huge fiasco. . . . where in the '80s, it's a backyard competition. Very few banners, and it's all just the competitors, their friends, the sponsors, and a few photographers from the magazines. . . . So it was grassroots. It was VIP. No audience. It's an underground scene. It was so backyard. If you knew where it was, you could come. And wherever you're at, the guy's like, 'I can't believe they're all here at my house.'"

Despite ups and downs with some of the biggest companies—he rode for Powell, Dogtown, Vision, Sims, and Santa Cruz, among others—the '80s were Hosoi's heyday, his coming of age. With his roots anchored in concrete and his fear dissolved by his desire to be the best, Hosoi pushed skateboarding higher than anybody—period—literally shaking a

ALL OF THE '80S WERE CHRISTIAN'S HEYDAYS. HE WAS ALWAYS THE BEST. BACK IN THE '80S, IT TOOK YEARS OF PRACTICE TO BECOME A PRO. BUT SOMETHING WEIRD HAPPENED IN THE '90S—STREET SKATING, A KID COULD BECOME PRO IN LIKE A YEAR, SIX MONTHS. GUYS LIKE CHRISTIAN AND TONY HAWK JUST GOT LOST IN THE MIX, AND THE COMPANIES TURNED THEIR BACK ON THE VERT PROS AND WENT WITH THE NEW SCHOOL. IT CHANGED OVERNIGHT. THE WHOLE INDUSTRY CHANGED. CHRISTIAN'S MAKING TONS OF MONEY ONE DAY, SKATEBOARDING, BEING A SUPERSTAR, AND THEN OVERNIGHT, THE KIDS WOULD HAVE NO RESPECT. ALL OF A SUDDEN THE KIDS WERE LOOKING AWAY. YOU KNOW, IT WAS HARD. YOU PUT YOUR WHOLE LIFE INTO IT AND ALL OF A SUDDEN SOME LITTLE KID YOU'VE NEVER HEARD OF—WHO CAN'T EVEN REALLY SKATE—IS SELLING MORE BOARDS AND MAKING MORE MONEY

EDDIE REATEGUI

ramp to its foundation as he pumped more and more speed from increasingly higher aerials. Launching from the lip with the speed of a downhiller, Hosoi blasted fluidly and with unmistakable control waaaay over the heads of skaters waiting their turns on deck before tweaking his body and board stylishly in mid-flight and setting it back down perfectly, his wheels just below the lip, his arms down at his sides, his expression a portrait of confidence and thrill.

"In the '80s, not a lot of people really liked Hawk's style because he was kind of a small, skinny little kid and he did tricks differently then everybody," Dave Duncan remembers. "Whereas Christian flew higher than anybody and he had more style than anybody, more grace and finesse. Everybody would be like, 'Wow, if I could just fly like Christian . . .'

"Tony Hawk was more of a trickery guy, like he did these, what we called circus tricks back then, which was not so much the roots of skateboarding, the soul. Kind of like when you look at surfing, it's all about style, cuz there's not a lot of tricks you can do on a surfboard, so it's all about your style, and that's where Christian was keeping with the roots of skateboarding, with the style. He didn't do the circus tricks like Hawk, the varials and the finger-flips and that kind of weird stuff. Christian never really did a lot of that. Christian did high ollies and late tail-grabs and had just lots of hang time over your head. I mean, I skated with him and he's over my head. I was like, 'Wow, I wish I could fly that high.' But, you know, as much as you practice and practice, nobody could fly like Christian."

"You know, to this day," Duncan continues, "when you read interviews in *Transworld* or *Thrasher* or whatever, guys are asked, 'Who's your favorite skater?' And they say, 'Oh, Christian Hosoi, without a doubt, was one of my main influences.' Not only that, but Christian could skate everything. He could ride streets, he could ride the pools, and he could do it all with style. And he could do it all better than anyone else. You know, he could win the street contest, then go win the vert contest. Or be the best guy in the pool session and win the longest carve."

CHRISTIAN'S FOLKS, IVAN AND BONNIE, both born and raised in Hawaii, met in college on the North Shore. Ivan surfed and studied art. Bonnie took business classes. When Ivan landed a scholarship to the Chouinard School of Arts (forerunner of CalArts), they moved to Los Angeles, where they postponed having a baby until after graduation. Christian was born October 5, 1967, and when he was just a few months old, the family moved to Berkeley, where Ivan had been accepted into a master's program at the university.

Christian wasn't one for crawling, remembers Bonnie, and once he got to his feet, at ten and a half months, he instantly started climbing everything in sight. When he was eleven months, she caught him standing on the toilet-seat lid, heading for the tank. When he was eighteen months, other mothers would scold her for being negligent when toddler Christian climbed to the top of the highest jungle gym in the park. In grade school, when the other kids bugged him, he'd scale thirty feet to the top of a playground tree and just sit there until his teacher called his parents to come talk him down. Ivan would show up and take pictures of him.

"He knew his center, and he just had to go high," says Bonnie, now remarried and living on the East Coast. "He always had to go higher and higher."

"He was never afraid of heights," adds Ivan, who lives and works at City Lights church in Santa Ana. "Shoot, heights were his thing."

When Christian was seven, Ivan remembers, the family chased work back to Hawaii. Ivan's good friend sent Christian a set of Cadillacs (skateboarding's first urethane wheels) and a set of Chicago trucks for his birthday. But no board. So Ivan built him one in the shaping room where he formed and repaired his own surfboards. Roughly two feet long and four or five inches wide, with a Gerry Lopez lightning bolt on top, the red fiberglass board had an upturned nose and a downturned tail, which, Ivan figured, his son could lean back on as a brake. Christian rode it backward, finding the upturned nose to be better suited as the tail. Neighborhood girls yelled, "All clear!" making way for Christian as he butt-bombed the steep street that ran past their home.

The family was back in Los Angeles by 1975, where Ivan built Christian a short quarter-pipe in the art studio where he did custom carpentry alongside art-school buddy Mike Murray. Murray's son Aaron was the same age as Christian, and they skated together pretty much every day. Aaron "Fingers" Murray would also go on to make a name for himself in skateboarding.

A few years later, Ivan and Bonnie separated, and Ivan focused on spending as much time with his son as possible. "I'd take him anywhere he wanted to go," Ivan remembers. "And he's into skating, so—bam!—every day after school we'd go to the parks. Big O. Marina. Skateboard World. He was so into it. I'd just let him guide me." Not long after Marina opened, Ivan landed a job as its park manager.

It's a golden memory for Christian: "I'm only ten years old, eleven now, and I'm getting really good. My first year there, I was already like the best small-bowl skater there was. Haven't gone to the big, deep pools yet. So [my dad] goes over there and he says to the guy, 'Yep, the owner sez I can work here and that I can be the manager of the place.' So now he's manager and I'm going, 'You're kidding, right? This is a dream come true.' Now I'm going there every single day. And I

IVAN HOSOI (RIGHT) COACHES GARRETT CAMPBELL THROUGH
THE DROP, SUNSET BEACH, NORTH SHORE, HAWAII, 1960
PHOTO COURTESY OF IVAN "POPS" HOSOI

open up the place. Sweep out the bowls. All the pinball machines, video games that I wanted to play. The snack bar was mine. The pro shop was mine. I was in there just running the whole place. And everybody's like, man, you're gonna be good when you get older. And I think that was pretty much the motivation and support I needed—the encouragement to pursue skateboarding [as] a lifelong career.

"And basically, the turning point was when I was just skating the bowls, and now I'm riding for Z-Flex. Jay Adams took me over to his dad's place in Venice, and I got on the team and I got free boards, free wheels, free everything. Tracker was flowing me free trucks. Vans was giving me free shoes. Rector was on the verge of giving me free pads, but since my dad was running [Marina skatepark] I could get pads for basically nothing through the skate shop. So basically, I'm shop-sponsored right off the get-go. . . . The same summer, Ted Terrebone came down and talked to my pops and goes, 'You know what? I wanna take a picture of your son.' And my father's all, 'Oh, awesome.' And he comes over and says, 'We're gonna do a photo session,' and I'm all, 'This is cool!' And then I got my first picture in *Skateboarder*. It was right before *Skateboarder* turned to *Action Now*, and I had a full-page color shot and I'm like, 'No way, I'm not in here, am I?' And I look again and, yep, it was me. And that was it—that was probably like the turning point. I mean, I couldn't even skate a deep pool yet; this was prior to me even graduating into being a man in skateboarding. I was still a little kid."

Christian turned pro at thirteen.

WITH TYPICAL REAL-LIFE courtroom tedium, Hosoi's case was dragged under by delays. After his July 11, 2003, resentencing before sympathetic Judge Kay, Hosoi had hoped to walk within a week. But by month's end, as prosecutors challenged Kay's call, a string of postponements had bumped his day in court to September, then to December, then into 2004.

> ALL THESE YOUNG KIDS HAD TAKEN OVER, YOU KNOW: IT WAS ALL ABOUT THIS NEW STYLE OF SKATING AND SMALL WHEELS AND BAGGY PANTS AND THE WHOLE HIP-HOP THING. IT JUST CHANGED SKATING, SO THERE REALLY WAS NO ROOM FOR THE OLDER SKATERS. BUT DURING THOSE TIMES, THERE WASN'T A LOT OF MONEY, SO CHRISTIAN . . . I THINK HE STARTED DABBLING IN THE DRUGS THERE JUST OUT OF DEPRESSION ALMOST. JUST KIND OF EXPERIMENTATION, MAYBE. YOU KNOW, LIKE KIND OF NOTHING TO LOSE
> DAVE DUNCAN

Back on the mainland, nerves stretched thin, and facing upward of ten grand in lawyer fees, Jennifer got on the phone. Within a few days, she put together a benefit night at a Huntington Beach cantina. Ten bucks at the door, all proceeds toward Hosoi's legal tab. Her timing was good: the three-day Vans Triple Crown Soul Bowl Expression Session was going down on the Huntington waterfront, and most pros were in town, many of them Hosoi's contemporaries. Plus, drawn by the pro pileup, mobs of skateboarders and people who like to hang out with them lined up in the parking lot as bands set up inside and early comers lounged in the VIP room, drinking free cans of Pabst Blue Ribbon, the unofficial beer of skateboarding. By 10 P.M. the place was packed.

Former Marina del Rey skatepark local Pat Ngoho's at the bar telling stories of how Hosoi, Mike Smith, and himself, as amateurs, could blow away any out-of-town pro who came to ride their home park. Seventies talent George Orton's setting the record straight

Santa City
No. 1850
MEMBER NUMBER
NAME Christian Hosoi
PHONE 932-5736
EXPIRES 81

00343 Hosoi (first) Chris
Additional fee to use facility without this membership card.
Expiration Date 10-28-79 Approved by CB
MARINA SKATEPARK
Membership Card

Temp. I.d.
Christian
HOSOI
10-5-67

sparks SKATEPARKS
Non-Member
Member
HOSOI, CHRISTIAN
Home Park   Exp. Date
GOLETA 4-11-80
I.D. # 1601 Signature
Christian

big O SKATEPARK
Christian Hosoi
Add. 3rd Ave.
City LA   Ph. 932-5336
Signature   Number 8949 Exp. Date 9-81

ENDLESS WAVE
SKATE PARKS
Bakersfield   Oxnard
Phoenix
Good until revoked
CHRISTIAN R. HOSOI
MEMBER
MEMBER'S SIGNATURE Christian
CLASSIFICATION A12
9 10 78 4417
DATE   I.D.

SKATEBOARD WORLD
5210 Faculty Ave., Lakewood, Ca 90712
Christian Hosoi 10
NAME   AGE
1875
MEMBER NO.   OR GUEST
10-14-79 10-5-67 732-533
EXPIRATION DATE BIRTHDATE PH. NO.
X Christian
SIGNATURE
SAFETY GUARDIAN (if under 18 yrs old)

skatetown SKATING LICENSE
MUST BE PRESENTED TO OPERATE A SKATEBOARD AT
aloha skatetown
29525 CANWOOD STREET
AGOURA, CA. 91301
213/889-5242
I agree to skate by the rules
and to help make
SKATETOWN A SAFETOWN.
X Christian
Signature
3853

skatetown SKATING LICENSE
MUST BE PRESENTED TO OPERATE A SKATEBOARD AT
aloha skatetown
29525 CANWOOD STREET
AGOURA, CA. 91301
213/889-5242
I agree to skate by the rules
and to help make
SKATETOWN A SAFETOWN.
X Ivan Hosoi
Signature
3852

Temp. I.a.
HOSOI
Ivan
9-26-42

NOW I WOULD SAY THAT I APPRECIATE EVERYTHING, WHERE BEFORE I TOOK IT ALL FOR GRANTED. AND I HOPE THAT MY TESTIMONY IS GONNA . . . LEAD PEOPLE TO NOT TAKE FOR GRANTED THE THINGS THEY HAVE. BECAUSE WHEN THEY'RE TAKEN FROM YOU BY MAKING A MISTAKE, LIKE THE ONE THAT I'VE MADE—YOU KNOW, MY DRUG ADDICTION MADE ME MAKE A BAD DECISION, AND I HAVE TO PAY FOR IT. AND NOW THAT I KNOW HOW BAD SIN IS AND HOW BAD DRUGS ARE, I DO HAVE TO PAY IN PENALTY AND I DO HAVE TO PAY THAT DEBT. BUT I'M PAYING IT JOYFULLY. AND I HAVE THIS JOY IN MY HEART. . . . WHEN YOU HAVE THE ANOINTING OF THE HOLY SPIRIT COME INTO YOUR HEART AND CHANGE YOU AND MAKE YOU A NEW MAN, THOSE THINGS—I COUNT EVERYTHING THAT I HAVE LOST FOR THE EXCELLENCY OF KNOWING CHRIST NOW. AND TO ME IT'S WORTH EVERY MINUTE THAT I'VE SPENT HERE IN PRISON
CHRISTIAN HOSOI

about who *really* did the first frontside air (it was him, he says, not Tony Alva). Dave Duncan's cooling down on the patio out back, shaking his head with beaming disbelief at the afternoon's Grandmasters (thirty-six and up) finals jam at the Soul Bowl; in nearly three decades of skateboarding, he's seen few sessions go down with such cutthroat suspense and passion. Jennifer's working the door, trying to pull donations from everybody trying to get in for free, many of whom were not even born when Hosoi turned pro.

By 11 P.M., Jennifer's legal fund has breached the two-thousand-dollar mark, and the cantina's full of a scene that's distinctly Orange County: where a guy's out of place if his hat's not on crooked; where a girl doesn't blend in if she lacks a trendy tattoo riding the crack of her ass above low-cut jeans. Some band from the backwoods of Huntington Beach gets the crowd stomping and hooting, though one skeptical onlooker swears they'd sound better if they had spent as much time practicing as they did decorating the stage with redneck kitsch.

Between bands, the emcee raffles off "Free Hosoi" T-shirts and a few grab bags of goodies donated by prominent skateboard shoe companies. He also parts with a very limited-edition Hosoi skateboard deck, still in the plastic, the kind of sought-after product that many now consider far more valuable as a museum piece than as a well-shaped piece of maple to actually stand on and ride. A tall, pretty gal produces the winning ticket and claims her prize. Almost immediately a few hawks wave twenty-dollar bills at her, but she knows what she's got and she's not selling. Above her, tacked over the stage, a handmade banner reads, "Celebrate a legend."

Hosoi would count it a blessing—one of many incalculable gifts from God—that collectors covet pieces of his history. Half an ocean away, three hours behind, and locked down inside Honolulu's Federal Detention Center as the cantina benefit carries on toward midnight, Hosoi's likely reading his dog-eared bible, returning to a passage he says helps him through each day. It's from James: "Blessed is the man that endureth temptation: for when he is tried, he shall receive the crown of life, which the Lord hath promised to them that love him."

He falls asleep, alone with his dreams—his wife, his son, his mother and father, his friends, and the open sky above his next session.

CHRISTIAN'S FIRST MAGAZINE SHOT, *SKATEBOARDER*, JUNE 1980, MARINA DEL REY SKATEPARK
PHOTO: TED TERREBONE

THE '90s (WFO)

A 1968 GTO SITS IN THE SHADOWS DOWN A DIRT DRIVEWAY IN A QUIET NEIGHBORHOOD OF PORTLAND, OREGON.

PREVIOUS:
JESSICA STARKWEATHER FRONTSIDE-GRINDING
THE PUNK WALL,
BURNSIDE SKATEPARK,
PORTLAND, OREGON, JUNE 2003
PHOTO: JOE HAMMEKE

NEXT:
ELLEN BERRYMAN DOES A DAFFY DURING JETHRO TULL'S
"TOO OLD TO LIVE" TOUR, L.A.
COLISEUM, 1976
PHOTO: JIM O'MAHONEY

SHE'S A BLACK-ON-BLACK BEAUTY POWERED BY A BIG-BLOCK 455.

Reflected in her shiny quarter panel, a small group of young women hangs out nearby, lounging and chatting on a big blanket in the grass. The afternoon's host, Jessica Starkweather, twenty-six, is pouring strong daiquiris straight from the blender pitcher. A friend asks Starkweather for the keys to the GTO. "You can't drive," Starkweather replies, "but let's go—I'll take you for a ride." They climb inside. The muscle car's motor thunders to life. Three daiquiris deep and on a suspended license, Starkweather lights 'em up down the street, heading for the freeway. Through town, pedestrians and motorists double-take on the tall, blue-eyed strawberry blonde driving the hot rod. Clicking on the tape deck, Starkweather banks onto the Fremont Bridge over the Willamette River. Windows rolled down, Ted Nugent's "Stranglehold" blasting from blown speakers, Starkweather opens her up, hitting 110 in the fast lane as the late-afternoon summer sun spills sideways across city and water.

If Starkweather's dead father, Fritz, is looking down (or perhaps up) from someplace otherworldly, he must certainly be proud. That's how the Vietnam vet raised his little girl, at full throttle. She remembers the go-cart he bought her and how, at four years old, she'd bomb the biggest hills from the top as boys twice her age chickened out halfway up. She swears she was just nine or ten years old when she took over the steering wheel from her drunken daddy and sweet-talked them through a late-night roadside checkpoint. She was on board, too, as the family fished commercially for salmon off southern Oregon's rugged coast. She also worked alongside him in the summer, logging the mountainous family acreage outside Gold Beach, where she was born. She jumped in on long road trips to biker parties with the Dirty Dozen. And she thought it a bit odd but fitting when he traded his '92 Harley Springer softtail for a green Kawasaki ZRX 1200R and proceeded to shatter his own land-speed records.

His fatal crash came on November 4, 2001, as he tried to kiss the sky on a Gold Beach airfield. When family members retrieved the Kawasaki, its speedometer was stuck at 135. He was 57, and before he went, he taught his daughter that, as far as motors go, bigger is better. As far as speed goes, faster is funner. As far as life goes, he'd say, it's best lived on the edge,

where the view, like the throttle, is always WFO. Wide fuckin' open.

RAISED MOSTLY BY HER MOTHER near the tall mountains outside Ashland, Oregon, Starkweather learned to ski when she was four. A decade into it, she took up snowboarding and never looked back, a typical transition for many longtime skiers in those days. Now sidestance on the slopes (in many respects a more comfortable, carving ride than one cluttered with skis and poles), Starkweather became quite content and confident with the sheer speed and big air so common to snowboarding. Out of high school in 1994, she moved north to the bigger mountains outside Portland.

Like many of today's female skateboarders, Starkweather crossed over from snowboarding, adding to the rapidly expanding circles of women skaters all over the world, from the Northwest to Florida, from Brazil to Australia. Indeed, the en masse influx of girls and women into skateboarding was perhaps its most conspicuous and interesting personality trait during the '90s.

To be sure, there have always been female skateboarders, even in the earliest eras. In the '60s, national teams, such as Hobie, featured women riders. In the '70s, women competed (typically in freestyle, that most gymnastically graceful of contest events, and in slalom) in their own divisions and could be found at most skateparks. But for virtually all of the '80s—as easy-access skateparks became a thing of the past, backyard vert-ramp riding took over, and punk rock replaced what's now called classic rock as the soundtrack of most sessions—skateboarding was, with very few exceptions, entirely male-dominated. The '90s, however, unfolded differently. Call it Girl Power. Call it boredom. Call it the tomboy revolution. Call it a

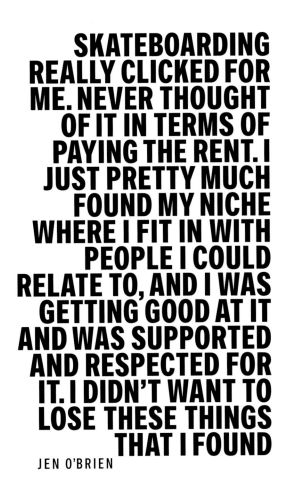

SKATEBOARDING REALLY CLICKED FOR ME. NEVER THOUGHT OF IT IN TERMS OF PAYING THE RENT. I JUST PRETTY MUCH FOUND MY NICHE WHERE I FIT IN WITH PEOPLE I COULD RELATE TO, AND I WAS GETTING GOOD AT IT AND WAS SUPPORTED AND RESPECTED FOR IT. I DIDN'T WANT TO LOSE THESE THINGS THAT I FOUND

JEN O'BRIEN

breakdown of tired stereotypes. Call it the influence of snowboarding. Call it a bit of all of the above.

For Starkweather, it happened on Mount Hood, where the warm-season snowboard camp featured wood skateboard ramps. She watched one of the other girls skate and was inspired, slowly picking up the basics on a borrowed board. Soon enough on her own board, a beat-up hand-me-down from some dude, she moved her passion from snowboarding (which she was getting burnt on, anyway) to skateboarding.

She quickly fell into the scene, coming off the mountain to ride Portland's Burnside skatepark and hopping in with other women skateboarders on long road trips to spots around the Pacific Northwest. On one such trip, she hit it off with Mike Swim while skating a homemade backyard bowl in Swim's hometown, Seattle. They eventually married, and, on September 23,

WENDY BEARER WITH BROTHER DANNY, PAUL REVERE JUNIOR HIGH, SANTA MONICA, CALIFORNIA, 1965
PHOTO: JAMES GREGORY

ABOVE:
JUDI OYAMA, HEAT WAVE SKATEPARK, MODESTO, CALFORNIA, CIRCA 1975
PHOTO: MIKE GOLDMAN, COURTESY OF JUDI OYAMA

RIGHT:
KERRIE COOPER, NORTH SHORE, HAWAII, 1978
PHOTO: DAN DEVINE

I ATE IT, I WALKED IT, I TALKED IT, I SHIT IT. I WAS TOTALLY CONSUMED BY SKATEBOARDING

JENNIFER LARSON
(FORMERLY JENNIFER JOHNSON), '70S SLALOM RACER

1998, they had a little girl, Sophia. Baby on her arm, Starkweather traveled with Swim extensively during the late '90s as he worked for Dreamland Skateparks, building world-class parks in rural towns around the Northwest, plus one in Austria. Their marriage was strained by this vagabond lifestyle and they separated after about four years. Swim stayed on the road, visiting his daughter between parks and on long holidays. Starkweather moved back to Portland, where she enrolled Sophia in school, landed a cocktailing job, and meshed back into the skate scene thriving beneath the Burnside Bridge, where she credits Tanya Golden as one of her original influences.

BORN IN SEATTLE AND RAISED IN THE HILLS on the fringes of North Plains, outside Portland, Golden grew up on the family farm. Helping out across roughly fifty acres, Golden harvested hay and peaches and tended cows, chickens, ducks, turkeys, rabbits, and a horse. Free time sent her on long explorations through the surrounding forests, and she'd return with pockets full of wild berries. But her mom would say no eating until after she'd double-checked for poison, keying out the berries in a botany book. Golden also spent a lot of time playing with her little brother, John.

"I could, A, stay home and play with dolls or, B, go out and ride motorcycles with my brother and his friends," she remembers. "Let's see, option A: dolls. No thanks."

By the time she was in junior high, she'd learned to keep up with the boys, and skateboarding came into her life as a few of her guy friends picked it up during the mid-'80s boom. "I used to steal the boys' boards and try and go ollie," she says. "I never got very proficient at ollieing, but I fell in love with downhilling. I lived on a hill. Downhilling was a necessity. And I just liked the rush from going fast." (To this day, nearly two

decades later, Golden still bombs the hills of Portland, "especially when the shit's hitting the fan in my life," she says. "I just focus in, and it clears my head.") After poaching the boys' boards for a while, Golden finally bought her own, a used set-up from some guy at school. Forty bucks got her a Santa Cruz Claus Grabke (with pink Tracker trucks and red Bullet wheels), a Suicidal Tendencies *Join the Army* cassette, and a duffel bag. She hid her board in the barn—from her dad, mainly—sneaking out after dinner to skate back and forth across the concrete foundation.

Out on the roads, pushing for miles from spot to spot, Golden and her skater boys would bomb hills and hit up the chunked-out Frisky Banks (down at the cat-food company) and the "sort of smooth, but not really" Worm Bank. Halfway through high school, she jumped in a car headed to town and first laid eyes on the crude beginnings of the now-legendary skatepark tucked away in the underbelly of Portland's Burnside Bridge. "It looked amazing," she remembers. "I was like, 'Holy shit!'"

She immediately set out to skate Burnside as much as she could, taking the bus into town in the morning, riding before school, and making it back before first

I THINK THAT WAS REALLY WHAT GOT ME INTO IT.... I WANTED TO SKATE BETTER THAN MY BROTHER
JUDI OYAMA, CONTEMPORARY SLALOM RACER

period (most of the time). Once she got her license, trips to Burnside became more frequent and much easier. So did cutting class. But she maintained good grades, took courses at Portland City College, and was an accomplished athlete (swimming, track, cross-country), so the ladies in the admin office would let her slide, she says. "They'd be like, 'Oh, so what is it today? Flat tire? Alternator? Ran out of gas? Locked your keys in the car?' And I'd be like, 'Oh, yeah, one of those.'" Inevitably, she says, most everything else fell by the wayside. Skateboarding took over. "I hate it when people tell me what to do," she explains. "I just didn't want to run track anymore. Skating was funner and the people were funner. It felt a lot better, so I did it."

But it wasn't easy. For years Golden, now twenty-eight, was one of the very rare girls who skated Burnside frequently. Her formative years at the park unfolded in an era virtually devoid of female skate-boarders. Back then, gal skaters weren't widely accepted, as they are now. "Oh, yeah, I got hassled by the guys," she says. "I had some guys tell me straight to my face that girls should not skate. And that just drove me even harder. But the guys who were really down for skating, they saw I was hungry for it. They didn't care. But they weren't gonna go any easier on me. They were stoked watching me slam, like anybody else.

"I've got a lot of respect for all those [Burnside] guys, but sometimes I've hated them so much [I've sworn] I'd quit skating and never go down to the park again. They'd just heckle me—just being dickheads. I don't know, just being a young teenage girl and wanting to skate and having crushes here and there, and I don't know—them just being dicks. I'd be all, 'Fuck you, dude! I'm never coming back!' And I'd be back the next day.

"And when one or two or three girls are there, it's like finally you've got a partner. When's there's just a few girls, it's like, 'Yeah, sista, wassuuuup?' Like, 'Cool, I got a girl to hang out with and we can talk shit in the

> ## I'VE SEEN THE ANALOGIES BETWEEN SKATING AND LIFE— LIKE HOW THEY REQUIRE COMMITMENT, PATIENCE, AND PERSISTENCE, AND HOW SOMETIMES THINGS MAY BE DISCOURAGING. BUT OTHER TIMES, THINGS COME TOGETHER AND IT MAKES YOUR DAY, AND FINDING THE FLOW THROUGH IT ALL IS A MUCH NICER WAY TO LIVE
>
> PEGGY OKI

corner while those guys are talking shit to us, but now there's two of us and we can handle it, you know?' And the girls hype each other up and the guys can go, 'Yeah, chicks! C'mon!'

"But when there gets to be a big group of girls, I'll leave. You know, when men skate together, I've never heard guys go, 'Oh, I can do *this*. What can you do?' Like if a guy said that, everyone else would be like, 'Yeah, whatever. Shut up.' And the guy gets heckled. But sometimes, when there're a lot of girls, they'll stand there and the hip will go out and the chin will go up and they'll be like, 'I just learned *this*. What can you do?' And it's like, ew, yuck, I don't want that. I did competitive sports for way too long to deal with that shit anymore. I quit running, I quit swimming. I quit it all

CAN I PLEASE JUST

GO REALLY FAST?

THERESA HUSTON,
BURNSIDE LOCAL

ABOVE:
HOLLY DEVEREUX, VAGABOND POOL, FRESNO, CALIFORNIA,
NOVEMBER 2002
PHOTO: RHINO

RIGHT:
EDIE ROBERTSON, TEA GARDENS, SANTA BARBARA, CALIFORNIA,
MARCH 1977
PHOTO: TOM SIMS

I HAD NO IDEA THAT THERE WERE GIRL SKATERS IN THE '60S AND '70S. WE THOUGHT WE WERE THE ONLY ONES. IT WAS JUST FUN, AND IT TURNED US ON TO THE PUNK SCENE. SKATING GOT US OUT OF THE SUBURBS AND BROUGHT US TO THE CITY TO SKATE AND SEE PUNK SHOWS. AND IT TOOK US ON GREAT TRIPS TO THE STATES, EUROPE, AND AUSTRALIA

KATIE PIASTA, CANADIAN
SKATEBOARDER

WHAT'S WRONG WITH SKATEBOARDING? IT'S TOO COMMERCIALIZED, TOO MAINSTREAM, TOO JOCK, TOO MUCH OF A SPORT NOW. A LOT OF KIDS NOW THINK IT'S ABOUT GETTING SPONSORED AND TURNING PRO. EVEN THE GIRLS ARE LIKE THAT. I ALWAYS THOUGHT IT WAS ABOUT HAVING FUN

CINDY GORSET, PACIFIC NORTHWEST SKATEBOARDER

because I love skateboarding. I love the freedom of it. I love not having to show people up or being shown up or having to prove myself. The only proof I have to give is that I want to do it. And with a lot of girls that shit happens—the rock-star image rocks out and chicks start partying with their cocks out and it starts sucking. That doesn't happen between the guys that much, but with girls there's more of a competitive spirit, I think."

IT'S SUNDAY MORNING, AUGUST 3, 2003, and Cara-Beth Burnside arrives at the Soul Bowl Expression Session as a few handfuls of female skateboarders, ages twelve to late twenties, are wrapping up their final warm-up runs in the twelve-foot-deep, fifty-foot-long wooden bowl shaped sort of like a bent capsule. Lyn-Z Adams, thirteen, has her frontside airs down pat. Twentysomething Nicole Zuck is throwing backside double-truck carve grinds through the corner. Brazilian Karen Santos, seventeen, pulls off a big bag of tricks with consistency. As the clock winds down on warm-up, Cara-Beth, thirty-four, pulls on her elbow and knee pads, fastens the strap on her pink helmet, and drops in. Her first warm-up run blows all the others away. Back-to-back 50-50 grinds, waist-high air over the hip, a slider to fakie to a big, clean fakie ollie hang-up. Cara-Beth, who's also one of the top professional female snowboarders, is untouchable on vert. Has been for two decades. Next contest, the judges should save her the hassle of finding a parking spot on a crowded Huntington Beach weekend and just mail her the thousand-dollar check for first prize.

The rest of the gals are there gunning for second place. With two heats of seven skaters, it's the biggest all-girls session the Soul Bowl has seen in five years on the road, a centerpiece of the Vans Triple Crown competition circuit. The only one absent is Florida-born Jen O'Brien, whose man, Bob Burnquist, is also one of the world's best.

The mood around the bowl is relaxed. Most of these girls know and have been competing against one another for years. When one takes a hard slam, a few others jump in to help her to her feet. Between runs, they chat on deck. They hoot and clap as twelve-year-old Ciara D'Agostino drops in on the extension, a plunge with as many feet of vertical as she is tall. They bang the tails of their boards against the lip for Cara-Beth, who's just pulled a Gay Twist, a 360-degree backward aerial. They tap their feet and amp themselves up on the loud music blanketing their Expression Session—Ramones, AC/DC, Mötley Crüe, and Blondie.

Starkweather's down from Portland. She's been competing for the past couple of years, and she typically ends up in the money, usually a slot or three behind Cara-Beth. Today, though, she's not feeling it. Sure, she stopped drinking early last night (at a late-night benefit party for imprisoned skate legend Christian Hosoi) but slept restlessly, cramped against her girlfriends on the floor at Soul Bowl emcee Dave Duncan's condo, where skaters from all walks have been flopping over the contest weekend. Still, though, her skating looks good, and as she carves every corner of the bowl, more set on hauling ass than on pulling off lots of tricks, Duncan announces to the crowd that in his half-decade of orchestrating Soul Bowl competitions, Starkweather's "one of the fastest" he's seen.

Must be something in her genes.

CARA-BETH BURNSIDE FLIES A BACKSIDE AIR OVER THE HIP OF THE SOUL BOWL, HUNTINGTON BEACH, AUGUST 3, 2003
PHOTO: DÉSIRÉE ASTORGA

ONE WOULD THINK IT'S THE INCESSANT TRAFFIC, SPEEDING THRONGS OF IT AT ALL HOURS, FLOUTING ROAD LAW, HONKING HABITUALLY, AND CONSTANTLY SWERVING FOR POLE POSITIONS AND PARKING SPOTS. BUT IT'S NOT.

Nor is it the swarm of pedestrians, powerwalking, jaywalking, stepping into traffic to flag cabs, the tourists pointing their noses at city maps and street signs and freezing like a herd in the headlights when anything on wheels cuts too close. One could also point to the soft and sticky warped asphalt of a melting summer's day. But it's not that, either. And what about the manhole covers, superheated by steamy depths and baked to branding temperature by scalding sun? Or the small and large chunks of construction debris littering the streets and sidewalks? Nope. Is it the weather? It must be the icy wind of fall or winter's bitter snow or spring's long run of thundershowers or the sweltering heat and humidity of August. Good guess, but no.

So what is it?

"The street skater's worst nightmare," says Steve Rodriguez, "is garbage juice."

And it's not just any old garbage juice. It's New York City garbage juice, oozing from grimy cracks in the wretched undercarriages of trash trucks that pulverize the rotting discards of eight million people crammed into five boroughs. It's stinky, it's slimy, it's downright deadly.

One night a few years back, Rodriguez was barreling down Broadway, enjoying the wind-in-the-face freedom and fast flow of a smooth stretch of street between Midtown and downtown. Approaching a light that he sensed was about to turn yellow, he stomped on it, kicking hard for the intersection. The light turned, and just as Rodriguez was about to soar

through the crossroads, he hit an invisible and massive slick of garbage juice. Traction gone, his board, as if hitting a patch of black ice, drifted sideways and out of control, pitching him to the slimy asphalt. The light turned red. Like a sunscreen-slathered kid on a Slip 'n Slide, Rodriguez lost little speed as he skimmed head-first into the intersection and a cab driver, also in tune with the lights, gunned from the cross street as his signal flicked green.

From the cabbie's perspective, the sight of Rodriguez's Pete Rose slide into the midst of a Broadway intersection must have been as odd as it was frightening. But luckily for Rodriguez, at that moment the cabbie's instincts trumped his bewilderment, and his right foot darted from gas pedal to brake. Rodriguez rolled away from his incoming death, and he came to a stop on his back as the cab's front tires screeched to a standstill, inches shy of squishing his head like a grape.

If skateboarders are even distantly related to alley cats, Rodriguez has certainly lost a life or two on the streets of New York City. Still, he's driven by curiosity, by the hunt, by a nearly fearless independence. Hypersensitive to his surroundings, Rodriguez, like most longtime skateboarders whose everyday views are dominated by cityscape, can read the streets like a lifelong surfer can read wind and sea. It's simply a matter of paying attention—close attention—to the traffic's red, yellow, and green, to the pedestrians' flashing crossing signals, to the reactions and intentions on the

BOBBY PULEO CATCHES A KICKFLIP
BETWEEN PLAYTHINGS ON A CHINATOWN SCHOOLYARD, MAY 2001
PHOTO: © ROBERICKSON
PREVIOUS:
STEVE RODRIGUEZ THRUSTS A FRONTSIDE WALL-RIDE BENEATH
THE BROOKLYN BRIDGE, SUMMER 2000
PHOTO: GERHARD STOCHL

faces of drivers and walkers and bikers, to dripping garbage trucks. Indeed, calling the most devoted and hardcore of street skaters an evolved hybrid of pedestrian and vehicle wouldn't be much of an exaggeration.

RODRIGUEZ'S EVOLUTION BEGAN IN 1984 in his hometown, Holmdel, New Jersey. A dedicated BMX racer decked out in the latest flash and armor, Rodriguez had his first taste of skateboarding when his best friend gave it a go. Rodriguez bummed his board and tick-tacked circles around his friend's driveway. That's all it took. Rodriguez was hooked. Within a few weeks, he had ditched his bike and all its accessories and started skating as much as possible. His first board was a fiberglass hand-me-down from his older sister. Every so often, he'd go surf Sandy Hook, a beach break in southeast New Jersey.

A few backyard ramps and indoor skateparks could be found not too far from Rodriguez's front door, but he always had the best time skating everything he could find along the way, namely curbs, steps, rails, banks, and parking blocks—all the treasured ingredients of a worldwide skatepark created by humankind's habit of building civilization with a concrete foundation. It wasn't long before the metropolis across the river became Rodriguez's pot of gold. By the time high school rolled around, he and his skater buddies were cutting class in the morning, hopping the train forty minutes into Manhattan, riding the city all day, and getting back home in time to check in with Mom before skating off into the evening. By the end of the '80s, he was getting free boards and shirts from Vision.

Rodriguez's big decision came in 1989: either skate fulltime with aspirations of turning pro, or go to college. He opted for the latter, enrolling at Ohio's

TO KEEP FROM GETTING BUSTED, YOU GOTTA JUST HIT AND RUN. DON'T SKATE ONE SPOT FOR TOO LONG
DAN PENSYL

Marietta College. "I had to get away from New York City," he says. "I knew if I went to NYU, I wouldn't go to school; I'd just skate and hang out with my friends." Between sports-medicine classes and freshman prerequisites, Rodriguez did manage to get away on the weekends to skate in Columbus, in Athens, Georgia, and in one of his favorite cities for skateboarding, Huntington, West Virginia. He also made it up into the hills to visit Brewce Martin's backwoods ramp compound and unofficial skateboard museum, Skatopia. Halfway through college, he switched majors to marketing and advertising, and immediately he felt more comfortable and familiar with the curriculum. "In high school I was always selling shit to kids," he explains. "I'd buy throwing stars from Asian World of Martial Arts and take them to school and sell them." He also peddled black-market fireworks he'd haggle from old men in dark Chinatown basements. "The city didn't scare me cuz I was always going there to skate," he says.

Rodriguez returned to New York with a college degree under his belt. It felt good to be back, but something was missing. The skateboarding scene and

THE BEST THING ABOUT SKATING IN NEW YORK COMPARED TO OTHER CITIES IS THAT IT'S PROBABLY ONE OF THE LAST PLACES ON EARTH WHERE THE COPS DON'T REALLY FUCK WITH YOU. THE COPS GOT BETTER THINGS TO DO. IN NEW YORK, THERE'RE WACKOS EVERYWHERE, AND NOBODY GIVES A CRAP IF YOU'RE SKATEBOARDING. EXCEPT FOR SECURITY GUARDS—BUT YOU JUST KEEP MOVING. AND THAT'S THE OTHER BEST PART: THE CITY'S LIKE A PLAYGROUND—SKATING TO SPOTS AND HITTING SPOTS ALONG THE WAY. IT'S LIKE ONE BIG LONG RUN. THE WHOLE CITY'S LIKE ONE BIG SKATEPARK

CHARLIE WILKINS

the companies that were part of it, he remembers, seemed watered down, diluted by too many sponsored skateboarders who were more into "looking cool and chillin'" than skateboarding. Rodriguez saw an opportunity, and in the mid-'90s he launched 5boro Skateboards out of his Greenwich Village apartment. These days, Rodriguez, thirty-two, still runs 5boro from the home office, and also stores boards and

PAUL McELROY STICKS A FRONTSIDE NOSEGRIND, OCEAN PARKWAY,
QUEENS, JUNE 2001
PHOTO: © ROBERICKSON

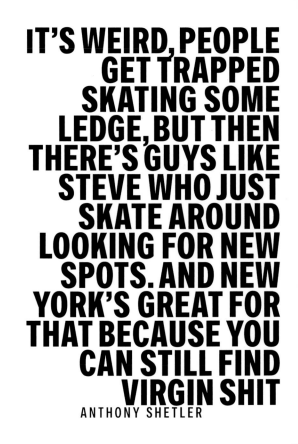

shirts and shipping supplies next door, sharing base-ment space with Avignone Pharmacy in a building his uncle owns. During a good month, Rodriguez sells about three thousand boards, impressive for a company that doesn't advertise in any of the major skateboarding magazines. He sponsors about a dozen riders, some of whom get free boards and shirts and a hot meal every so often, while others, such as Charlie Wilkins, get a decent paycheck and full health care.

THE BRICK TRIANGLE OF FATHER DEMO Square rests near the crossroads of Sixth Avenue and Bleecker Street in Greenwich Village. Joe's famous pizza pies bake thinly and crisply on the corner. Avignone Pharmacy stands across the street. Old ladies throw breadcrumbs to pigeons. A man with dreadlocks blasts reggae from a boom box as big as two fire hydrants. A smoker on a green bench rips open a $7.50 pack of Marlboro Lights. Professional skateboarder Charlie Wilkins, twenty-seven, and his wife, Victoria, thirty-two, both in town from Boston, sit and wait. It's just after 11 A.M. on a Sunday in the middle of June 2003. A solid week of rain and humidity has blown away, leaving the New York sky blue and cool.

Board in hand, Rodriguez steps from his well-kept sixth-floor apartment, slips on his shoes in the hall, rides the elevator to the ground floor, and skates to Demo Square, less than a block away. Wilkins and Rodriguez greet each other like old friends. A few minutes later, up rolls Justin Barnes, a bald but young-looking twenty-three-year-old with a jaw like a bull-dog's. Anthony Shetler, twenty, also arrives; he recently signed with prestigious Birdhouse, Tony Hawk's team. He's taking it easy, nursing a strained Achilles tendon. On his heels come friend Tim Rioux, nineteen, and last, on a board with big, soft, smooth-rolling wheels

and wearing a backpack bulging with camera equip-ment, nineteen-year-old Seamus Deegan.

Rodriguez leads the way as the group (minus Victoria, who's going shopping) pushes in a long line up Sixth Avenue, riding on the street, hanging to the right, where a bike lane would be. None of them takes the sidewalk—too rough, too many peds. Better off out in traffic, where the way is smooth and the cars and trucks and buses and bikes can see them coming and going. On the corner of Eighth Street and Mercer, at the foot of a miniature skyscraper, where anybody else would see only a plaza under extensive remodel—a scattering of lumber and hoses, an air compressor on a trailer chained to a railing—the group of skateboard-ers stares wide-eyed, as if at a Christmas tree knee-deep in presents. They draw mental lines of grinding and tail-sliding along concrete ledges of varying

DAN PENSYL SNAPS AN OLLIE FROM A TRAILER BED AND CARRIES IT CLEAN OVER A CONCRETE HIGHWAY
BARRIER BENEATH THE WILLIAMSBURG BRIDGE,
SOUTH FIFTH AND KENT, MAY 2001
PHOTO: © ROBERICKSON

heights and lengths, slick with waterproof lacquer. Wilkins says, "You know what else would be sick? Prop one of these pieces of plywood right here"—pointing at a low bench near a four-foot-tall wall between the plaza and the sidewalk—"and pop flips over that wall." Rodriguez is contemplating an ollie from the plaza to boardslide on the metal edge of the air compressor and down into the street. Deegan is unzipping his camera bag. But before ideas can turn into footage, a security guard appears from behind the mirrored glass of the lobby. "This closed," he says in his new language. "You leave now."

"C'mon," Rodriguez calls to the crew, "there's something else right up the street." And they're off to Fifth Avenue and West Thirteenth Street, where a looming, makeshift traffic sign stands roadside. Imagine a piece of plywood eleven feet tall and four feet wide, supported with two-by-fours and stabilized on one side with a slant of plywood wedging up from the street at a forty-five-degree angle and meeting the vertical plane about halfway up its height. Imagine pushing down the street against oncoming Fifth Avenue traffic and riding up the forty-five-degree slant on a skateboard. Near where the wedge meets the vertical, pop the skateboard's tail against the plywood, part company with it as it spins a complete revolution, land it, and roll backward down the angled junction and out into the street. That's what Charlie Wilkins does. It's called a kickflip fakie, and it takes him ten attempts as peds slow their Sunday strolls to take a gander, as buses and cabs race past and, as some cable TV producer across the street watches Wilkins's stunt and, in that transparently condescending tone a man assumes when he thinks he knows everything about something he knows nothing about, tells his friend, "This is the kind of extreme stuff we'll be providing with on-demand video."

Rodriguez is standing closest when a lady sees Wilkins take a fall. She almost yells at Rodriguez, "Do you know you could break your neck?!?" Rodriguez has heard it all before and, in his favorite response, he puts his face an inch away from hers, then cocks his head to one side like a perplexed dog and, staring at some faraway place, says, "What?!? Huh?!?" (Dealing with murderous motorists, however, is a different matter, and when a driver deliberately tries to run over Rodriguez and/or his skateboard, he'll skip the crazy routine, catch up to them at the next light, break their back windshield with his board, and wave at them and smile before skating away against traffic.)

After landing another kickflip, Wilkins steps it up, going for the 360 flip, and he's soon shirtless, sweating under the midday sun, his back streaked with gutter grease after a few tumbling bails. Deegan captures every attempt with his video camera, Barnes comes in with his own backside kickflip 180, and Rodriguez turns his encouragement toward a six-year-old girl trying to one-up the boys with her pink jump rope. She bets Rodriguez she can cleanly hop through ten con-

THE BEST THING ABOUT SKATING IS GOING SOMEPLACE. THEY SAY [IT] ABOUT A LOT OF THINGS, THAT THE BEST PART IS THE JOURNEY, NOT THE DESTINATION. IT'S EXACTLY LIKE THAT WITH SKATING
STEVE RODRIGUEZ

secutive turns before Wilkins can land his 360 flip. She does, and Rodriguez hands her a few 5boro stickers. Dozens of attempts later, Wilkins lands the 360 flip and rides it away clean like he's done it all his life. Just as Deegan is moving to pack away his camera, Barnes climbs to the top of the traffic sign and, balancing on a four-inch-wide piece of lumber eleven feet above the asphalt, calls for somebody to throw him his board. Deegan clicks on his camera; pedestrians stop cold and stare, but a few look away with the thought that something very, very terrible is about to happen. Barnes props the tail of his board against the wooden lip and steps on, free-falling six feet straight down to where the vertical ply meets the forty-five-degree bank to the street. For the most crucial instant, he's looking good—his feet are positioned properly, his body's not too far forward or back—and he sticks the landing, but his board is off by the slightest angle, causing it to shoot off into traffic. Barnes himself, however, maintains his heavy downward momentum, and his bulldog jaw bounces against Fifth Avenue. It's the toughest slam anybody has witnessed in a long time, and a long time passes before Barnes is on his feet. He's shaken but okay, smiles it off as blood pours from a deep gash in his right palm and his left elbow starts to swell. Deegan queues up the footage and passes around the camera so everybody can get a second wincing look.

They all take off back to the Village.

STILL A BIT GLAZED AND GREASY from a night of drinking till sunup—a barhopping sendoff for a skateboard brother bound westward on a long road trip—Dan Pensyl, twenty-five, is sitting alone in Father Demo Square sipping a rehydrating sports drink when Rodriguez and the rest arrive.

Growing up in Catasauqua, Pennsylvania, Pensyl started skateboarding in the third grade. "My neighbor across the alley had a board," he remembers, "and as soon as I saw him ollie up a curb, my mind was blown." His parents bought him the day's drugstore gem, a fluorescent-green Nash "Executioner" (its underside illustrated with a huge dragon sitting on a pile of skulls), and his dad took it outside, said, "Here, this is how you do it," and stepped on, thoroughly wilsoning (as when Mr. Wilson steps on Dennis the Menace's

misplaced skateboard), ending up on his ass. "I was hooked," Pensyl says. In fifth grade, he updated his ride to a Lance Mountain model he bought off the paperboy for fifteen bucks.

The skate scene in Catasauqua was surprisingly big at the time, Pensyl remembers, but was mostly filled with high school dudes who wouldn't let him ride their spots. "The older kids would throw me into the bushes and try and make out with my sister," Pensyl says. "They had a mini-ramp, but I wasn't allowed to skate it until high school." Until then he had to be content with the curbs and sidewalks surrounding two nearby churches.

Just out of high school, Pensyl often skated an indoor park in Hackettown, New Jersey. That's where he met Rodriguez. "I was trying to kickflip this pyramid," he remembers, "and Rodriguez, this grown man who looks like Conan, comes up to me and yells, 'Do it, you pussy!' Afterward he's telling me that he's starting a company but can't tell me the name of it yet." Rodriguez got Pensyl's phone number and three months later put him on the newly founded 5boro team as the company's first rider. Six years later, Pensyl's one of 5boro's top amateurs, an all-around ripper who attacks handrails and curbs with as much speed as he hits backyard pools and ramps. (His bowl-riding skills have improved vastly since he landed a job at Brooklyn's Owl's Head skatepark, where, between speed runs of his own, he watches over the kids and makes sure everybody's wearing a helmet.)

Pushing away from Father Demo Square, Pensyl and Rodriguez lead the way down Sixth Avenue, then bank west toward the Hudson River, weaving at speed through the smoggy standstill of honking traffic. Near Desbrosses and Canal, Rodriguez ollies up to the sidewalk, heading straight for a wide metal rolling door locked down over a city storage garage. Where it meets the base of the door, the sidewalk slants slightly

NO MATTER HOW LONG YOU'VE LIVED IN NEW YORK CITY, SKATING THROUGH TIMES SQUARE AT NIGHT IS STILL DOPE
BURTON SMITH, PRO

upward, somewhat smoothing out the abrupt ninety-degree transition. At the harsh juncture, Rodriguez unleashes a picture-perfect backside wall-ride: lifting his front wheels, bashing up the metal door, and riding the vertical surface a good two feet above the deck before turning on his back wheels and riding back to the sidewalk. Pensyl follows with his own, then Rodriguez's good friend Jamie Balling, a lanky redhead who's mysteriously materialized from some side street, does the same. The whole crew stops to session this metal door, riding up and back down it with the most incongruous and appropriate of skateboarding tricks — the wall-ride at once goes against skateboarding's smooth flow and falls in perfect lockstep with its boundless innovation. But above all, wall-riding, once mastered, is just plain fun. Tim Rioux gets a round of hoots as he rolls away smiling from the first one he's ever pulled off.

Back on the move, Rodriguez calls for the crew to follow him downtown, adjacent to the void where the Twin Towers once stood. "Oh," mumbles Pensyl, to himself mostly. "We're going to where I broke my leg — I ain't goin' anywhere near that spot."

On Labor Day Weekend 1998, grinding down a handrail since taken out with the wreckage of 9/11 — one of dozens of skate spots lost to terrorism — Pensyl came off his board at high speed and landed wrong on his leading (left) foot. His shinbone (tibia) splintered vertically, and his fibula broke twice, leaving a two-inch length of bone floating sideways between jagged ends. Tumbling to a stop, Pensyl lifted his busted limb. It

dangled in a horrible approximation of the human leg. "Ow," he remembers saying. "Guys . . . I think I fucked up my leg." After a speedy ambulance ride and an intricate four-and-a-half-hour operation, doctors were still worried that Pensyl might lose his foot as intense swelling all but shut down blood circulation. But after four days of monitoring, doctors gave him the good news: Pensyl could keep his foot. All told, he spent nine days in the hospital. Rodriguez visited him nearly every day. Two plates, twenty screws, sixty-five thousand dollars, and seventeen months of downtime later, Pensyl slowly started skateboarding again, and these days it's tough to tell if the accident has slowed him down at all.

The new handrails in the plaza where Pensyl snapped his limb get only quick looks from Rodriguez and the rest before the crew cuts east through narrow streets. An increased number of armed security guards — another bummer of post-9/11 New York — watches the plazas of nearly every major building downtown. Disappointed but not deterred, Rodriguez, Pensyl, and Jamie B. push out ahead of the rest and stealthily one-hit a few marble benches before vanishing around a street corner, way ahead of watchmen in pursuit. Down a few more one-way streets and around as many crowded corners, the crew at last rolls into the echoing underbelly of the Brooklyn Bridge.

Here are the famous Brooklyn Banks — one's a long, steep, smooth overhead slant of bricks swelling from one side of a downhill approach, the other a smaller but steeper bend of bricks lifted like a wave from a tipped plaza. Skated steadily since the '70s, these banks bore and bred many of the East Coast's greatest skateboarders, as well as countless unknown rippers. Fast and fun and big enough to make a skateboarder consider the bloody consequences of timid execution, the spot has lived long in the lore of skaters worldwide — indeed, no self-respecting skateboarder would visit the city and not ride the Brooklyn Banks. The spot's been so popular for so long, in fact, that at least one city parks commissioner has suggested officially

A SKATEBOARDER'S COLLECTION OF NO SKATEBOARDING SIGNS
PHOTO: LAURA KLEINHENZ

recognizing the banks as a place where skateboarders can do their thing, free from hassling security guards.

Another crew of skateboarders and a few BMX bikers have a session going already, and Rodriguez and the rest melt into the mix, giving out head nods with each pass. Starting from the top, Rodriguez pushes powerfully down the clattering brick—bikers making way—before cutting a hard right between two concrete planter boxes. He climbs the bank to its meeting with a broad, square pillar that drops from the belly of the bridge. At the harsh juncture, he jams into a towering wall-ride, arching across vertical concrete, then back down to brick, riding away with speed to spare. The others follow, carving their own lines, going bigger with every pass, for the moment sweating thrill from dull light and grimy shadows under the foot of one of New York's busiest bridges.

Back when he was a kid, Rodriguez would skate the banks for hours, but today he's on the move, pushing

his crew onward to a scattering of spots so that Deegan can collect a palette of footage for an upcoming 5boro video. So they leave the banks behind and recharge with thin slices and iced tea from a pizza joint on the outskirts of Chinatown.

The afternoon comes and goes.

The skateboarders hit more rails, more banks. The traffic moves in long pulses between lights. The skateboarders grab onto passing taxis and slingshot through intersections. The men with basketballs cuss and argue, and sometimes a game breaks out. The skateboarders smile at beautiful New York women with sun on their shoulders. The children share part of their playground with Pensyl as he tries to snap a double ollie up a short bilevel amphitheater. The skateboarders cool down in the shade of the park. The big man with the big boom box sways to some reggae. Deegan loads his van with skateboards and skateboarders and calls it a day. The man behind the counter at Joe's Pizza scoops a cup of Italian ice, half lemon, half cherry.

Rodriguez eats it slowly. Then he skates off alone, in the opposite direction from his apartment.

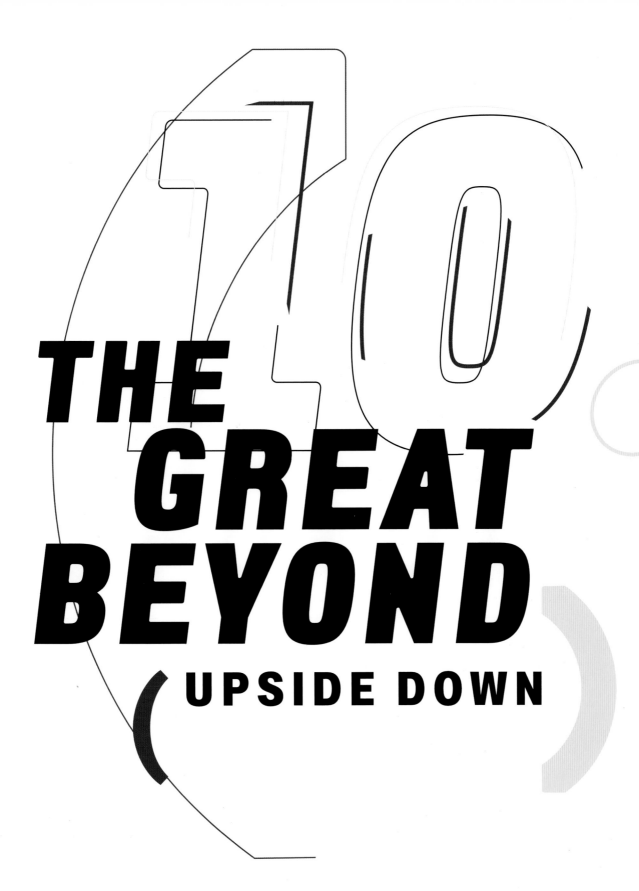

10

THE GREAT BEYOND

UPSIDE DOWN

BOB BURNQUIST WAS TEN YEARS OLD WHEN HIS SKATEBOARD, A STEEP HILL, AND GRAVITY CONSPIRED TO MAKE HIS NEXT SHOWER INTO A DEEPLY ETCHED MEMORY OF STINGING PAIN.

Sitting on his worn-out fiberglass rattletrap and facing down a pitted street in his hometown of São Paulo, Brazil, Bob lifted his feet and let the pull of gravity take over. An adrenaline junkie getting his fix, Bob surged with rabid joy through every second of rapid acceleration. Both feet pointed downhill and his arms down along his sides, he gripped the thin edges of his skateboard and, with what might be considered a semblance of control, leaned into turns. Then his front wheels dove into a deep crack in the pavement, yanking the board from beneath the boy. He was flung forward and came down face-first; the rest of his exposed flesh soon followed. Classic road rash.

From this first slam, Bob's skateboarding injury list stretched on impressively. His most memorable mishaps: two broken ribs from slamming against a metal handrail; multiply broken right elbow (five times at last count); two-bone break of right wrist and three snapped fingers on same hand (all from one crash), plus four or five more breaks to the same wrist, which is now reinforced with a metal pin; hyperextended right knee (captured on video in the skate flick *Brazilian Vacation*); bruised face and busted lips (from the first and second times, respectively, that he attempted dropping in on a vert ramp); and a concussion (which he actually can't remember but was told for certain did happen).

It wouldn't be precise to say skateboarders thrive on injury. Really, getting hurt is probably the worst thing about skateboarding, namely because bone breaks, hip contusions, ankle rolls, and bell ringers can keep a skater off his or her board for painfully long stretches. But at the same time, to paraphrase an old saying, that which does not kill a skateboarder only makes a skateboarder stronger. Indeed, skateboarders who have taken years, sometimes decades, of hard slams often get back on their feet tougher and more confident than before. Bob is no exception.

THE BABY OF A BRAZILIAN MOTHER and American father, Bob was born on October 10, 1976, in Rio de Janeiro. Growing up mostly in São Paulo, Bob started skateboarding at the age of ten. "A lot of people were skating at that time," he remembers. "I was a little kid trying to find something to do. We all played soccer in the neighborhood. Back then my asthma was a lot worse, so I was always the goalkeeper. So I was never really active. But then I let my friend borrow my soccer ball

and he lost it. I went to his house to get it, and he said, 'Uh, I don't have it. But you can have whatever.' So I looked around and found this little fiberglass skateboard. It sucked. It was loud and flexy. But it was fun and I had a good time and I showed interest, and then me and my dad went to the shop to get a real board." Young Bob picked out all the parts but wouldn't get them until his eleventh birthday, when he and his father assembled the board together.

Around this time, Bob's parents separated, leaving the young skateboarder at home with his mother and two sisters. Skateboarding became his bond to the guys, and almost every day he'd skate the big ramp at a skatepark three blocks from home. On weekends he'd visit his father in Rio, becoming a fixture of the scene surrounding the city's made-for-skating concrete pool, the infamous Rio Sul Bowl, riding his splintering birthday-present board until it ended up in traffic. "We'd go down the hill to get something to eat, and my board went into the street and got run over. I was bummed," he remembers. "But I still wanted to go to the parks, so I grabbed my sister's roller skates and skated with my buddies. I roller-skated until I got a new board. My skateboard buddies were like, 'What are you doing?' You know, the in-line skaters and skateboard cliques today just don't go together, but back then with the roller skaters, we hanged. There wasn't a

PREVIOUS:
THOUGH NO PHOTOGRAPHIC PROOF HAS YET SURFACED, WITNESSES SAY DUANE "THE MASTER OF DISASTER" PETERS WAS THE FIRST SKATEBOARDER TO PULL OFF AN UPSIDE-DOWN RIDE.
HERE, PETERS GIVES THE INFAMOUS DEATH LOOP A PRACTICE RUN.
IMAGE SCANNED FROM *SKATEBOARDER MAGAZINE*, VOL. 5, NO. 5, DECEMBER 1978
ORIGINAL PHOTOGRAPH BY JEFF RUIZ

BOB BURNQUIST AT THE
HOME OFFICE,
VISTA, CALIFORNIA, SPRING 2002
PHOTO: JON HUMPHRIES

rift." Bob rode on eight wheels for about six months, until one of his skateboard brethren offered to buy him a new skateboard if he'd come back into the fold.

Back on four wheels, Bob progressed like a prodigy and quickly earned a reputation for walking away from the hardest beefs—ever slam so hard your insides moved?—more determined than before. Soon he was getting free clothes from a local skate shop. Free boards came next, but they weren't of the cutting-edge—and exorbitantly priced—caliber that most American companies were churning out at the time. Brazilian products, Bob says, were "lower quality, much heavier. But we learned, we skated and had a good time." Looking back, Bob, along with many of his Brazilian contemporaries, can smile appreciatively: shoddy equipment and tough terrain, sure, but it was the kind of scene that would, a decade later, churn out world-class rippers.

"The thing about Bob," says *Thrasher* editor Jake Phelps, "is that he learned it on concrete and he learned it the hard way.

"I met Bob in Brazil when he was like sixteen years old," Phelps continues. "We went down to Brazil, and he followed us around everywhere we went. He didn't speak English very well, and all he wore was ratty jeans, ratty-ass shoes, no shirt. He was this skinny, long, lanky dude, switch-ollieing channels and shit. No pads. And I was like, 'Dude, who's this dude?' And John [Cardiel, a top pro,] was like, 'Uh, homeboy's really good, you know.' Then we skated Rio Sul with him, and he wore pads and he did switch roll-ins into the pool. And I was like, 'Dude, that's it, okay, the guy's obviously . . . he's the best.' And I came back and I told [top pros] Mike Frazier and Neal Hendrix and Tom

BOB'S A DIFFERENT BREED ALTOGETHER. HE JUST REALLY LOVES LIFE, AND HE'S ALWAYS LEARNING, WHETHER IT'S PLAYING MUSIC, SHOOTING PHOTOS, DOING ART, SKATING, FLYING AIRPLANES, OR READING SPIRITUAL BOOKS. HE JUST CAN'T SIT STILL. HE FEELS LIKE HE HAS TO BE LEARNING SOMETHING OR DOING SOMETHING, AND HE ALWAYS HAS TONS OF FRIENDS AND FAMILY AROUND
JEN O'BRIEN

Boyle and I was like, 'I've seen it, it's coming. I've seen it, the future, Bob Burnquist, he's comin'.' And they were like, 'No way, there's nobody better than us, impossible.'"

But Phelps was right: In May 1995, Bob virtually came from out of nowhere to bag the top trophy against the world's best at the annual Slam City Jam in Vancouver, Canada. Not only was Bob pulling off maneuvers many had never seen before; he skated half his runs switch-stance. For a skateboarder (or surfer or snowboarder), riding "switch" means swapping foot positions. For Bob, who normally rides with his right foot on the tail (which means he's "regular-footed"), riding switch means his left foot is on the tail ("goofy-

HAIRSPLITTERS WON'T CALL IT A TRUE LOOP, BUT KENT SENATORE (PICTURED) AND MANY OTHERS CERTAINLY GOT UPSIDE DOWN INSIDE THE CLEAR-PLASTIC CAPSULE OTHERWISE KNOWN AS THE TURNING POINT RAMP, MARINA DEL REY SKATEPARK, SUMMER 1980
PHOTO COURTESY OF KENT SENATORE
(WHO SAYS JIM LEGGETT TOOK IT, THOUGH LEGGETT DENIES IT)

AFTER A TWO-DECADE HIATUS, THE LOOP MAKES A COMEBACK, AND THIS TIME
TONY HAWK (PICTURED) CRAVING THE UPSIDE-DOWN CARVE. SECRETLY,
HAWK DISPATCHED FLORIDA-BASED RAMP MASTER TIM PAYNE TO A TIJUANA BULLR
TO BUILD A LOOP FOR AN UPCOMING VIDEO,
THE END, WHICH WOULD FEATURE HAWK PULLING THE FIRST LOOP IN TWENTY YEARS.
PETER HEWITT AND AL PARTANEN ALSO MADE IT, BUT THAT'S NOT IN THE VIDEO. JULY 19
PHOTO: ATIBA JEFFER

footed"). Analogies are numerous: It's like Tiger Woods smashing four-hundred-yard drives from the opposite side of the tee; it's like Nolan Ryan throwing one-hundred-mile-per-hour fastball strikes with his fielding hand; it's like Jay Adams (who surfs regular) pulling in and out of a howling barrel at Backdoor Pipeline while riding goofy; or, as Razorcake.com's Retodd puts it, "It's like masturbating with your other hand, except you may break your wrist if you do it wrong."

"I was the announcer at that [Slam City] event, and when we announced [Bob] the winner, he just couldn't believe it," remembers Dave Duncan, a former Alva-sponsored pro who now designs and builds state-of-the-art contest and demo ramps. "There he was on the deck with guys like Danny Way and Colin McKay, you know, legendary pros at the time, and he beat them all. It blew his mind. When Bob came on the scene, he came on with a bang. Boom!—he beat everybody because half of his run was switch-stance, and at that time he was farther ahead in the switch-stance skating than anyone else.

"And I just think that those Brazilian guys are hungry," Duncan continues. "It's kind of like they're underdogs. I'd say there's another ten to twenty Brazilian pros on the scene right now. I've been calling it the Brazilian Takeover. There's something about the Brazilians . . . they're hungry, they like to go fast, they like to have the speed and style, like kind of what skateboarding is all about."

BUT BOB ALMOST DIDN'T MAKE IT to that auspicious contest. Just a few years earlier, he had nearly turned his back on skateboarding altogether as he caved in to

> THERE'RE NOT THAT MANY SKATEBOARDERS OUT THERE REALLY BRINGING SOMETHING NEW. THEY'RE JUST SEEING WHAT YOU'RE SUPPOSED TO DO AND THEY DO IT, WITH MAYBE A LITTLE SLIGHT VARIATION. BUT A COUPLE DUDES JUST TOOK IT IN A WHOLE NEW DIRECTION. THOSE ARE THE GREAT SKATEBOARDERS— THE ONES THAT BROUGHT SOMETHING NEW AND DIFFERENT TO IT, AND BOB IS BY FAR ONE OF THEM
> LANCE MOUNTAIN

drug addiction. Though cocaine and its cheaper, more deadly distillation, crack, had permeated Rio, Bob favored tripping on glue, an escape he regarded as second only to skateboarding. "I skated and I didn't care about things around me; I wanted to get out. We'd skate and go to my friend's house and sniff glue. Started doing it more and lost a little of the edge on the skate side. That's when I went, 'Whoa, hold on.' When you sniff glue, you lose your balance, you lose everything. You're out. Then I'm like, okay, that's it, and I chose skateboarding. It was a choice: as I was sniffing glue, I had a bag and I had a choice. I was either going to pop the bag or keep sniffing glue. It was almost like I blew my vices into the bag and then I popped it. Then I totally lost all interest in sniffing glue ever again. From that moment on, I instantly stopped. That was around the time when skating was

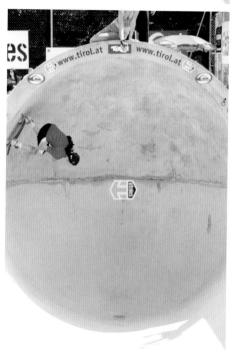

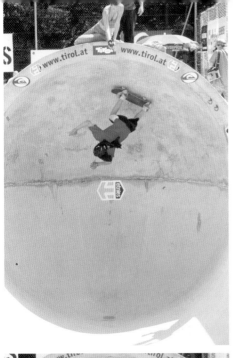
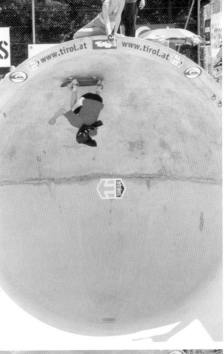

RATTENBERG SKATEPARK LOCAL (A.K.A. CRADLE BOY) CARVES THE CONCRETE CRADLE
BACKSIDE, AUSTRIA, JUNE 2002
PHOTOS: RHINO

on the up, and I really wanted to do it. But I'd still do some coke or drink. But there was always an action-reaction-type thing. I'd go out and party, then slam the next day. Then one night I stayed up all night partying, and we had a photo shoot [the next day]. And I started skating. I'm tired. I fell. Landed weird and buckled my knee, and that freaked me out. It felt like my knee came out of its socket. And the whole skating thing flashed before me. For two days I tripped on that. And I went into really deep prayer mode and I'm like, 'I'm done.' I asked for help. I really connected, and from that moment on, I was done with coke. I've never even felt like doing it again."

When Bob speaks of deep prayer and feeling connected, he's not herding himself into the corrals of some religion. "I'm not a religious person," he explains. "It's not a religion; it's more of like a way of thought, a way of thinking, an ideology. It's kind of like science and religion walking hand in hand. I'm a Christian Spiritist. We believe in reincarnation. We believe in the law of action-reaction and karma. The bible is not the word of God. It's the word of man,

written by man, but enlightened. In Spiritism, we read a lot of Alan Kardec, a French guy. He codified the Spiritist Doctrine. That's basically what I try to live by. But I'm not like, 'C'mon, everybody, be a Spiritist!'

"I was brought up with a little spirituality," he continues, "but I think it comes from before I was born. I think I've been around for a while. Not just in this life, but in successive lives. I got to the point at eighteen, nineteen where I felt mature already and really connected. And in Brazil the culture is a lot more open. When you talk about spirituality and reincarnation, people here [in the United States] instantly put their guard up: 'Oh, that's devil stuff.' You're not supposed to talk to spirits. All the apostles and Jesus, they're all mediums—that's why they were connected to the invisible. Brazil is really open to that form of Christianity, [one that] accepts mediums. I remember being kind of scared of spirits and my mom talking about them. But I remember liking to read, and so I started reading a lot and my mind really opened up. And that's where I feel confident, connected. I got faith. I mean, anything and everything that happens to me, it's just like, it's cool. All action-reaction. Like if I break my arm, that's fine, I'll take it and keep going."

Speaking of broken arms and mediums: "When I broke my wrist," he remembers, "I broke the two bones and three of my fingers and my arm was dangling real weird and that was the first time I went to a healer. She was close to the skatepark where it happened. I went there and she was talking to me and looking at my wrist, checking to see if she could fix it. So she's touching my wrist and checking it out and then all of a sudden she, like, yanks it and puts it into place without telling me or anything. She was being

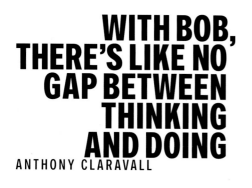

WITH BOB, THERE'S LIKE NO GAP BETWEEN THINKING AND DOING
ANTHONY CLARAVALL

THE ACHIEVEMENTS THAT BOB'S DONE LATELY WITH HIS LOOP AND THE ATTEMPT AT MOUNT BALDY WERE JUST, YOU KNOW, THINGS THAT I NEVER THOUGHT I'D SEE IN MY LIFETIME. SERIOUSLY, I MEAN, BACK IN '78 OR '79, I THOUGHT I'D SEEN IT ALL WHEN TONY ALVA DID A FRONTSIDE AIR IN A POOL. LIKE, "OH, MY GOD, HE'S IN THE AIR! WHAT ELSE CAN YOU DO? WHERE ELSE CAN YOU TAKE IT?" AND NOW THEY JUST SOMEHOW KEEP INNOVATING THESE TRICKS AND KEEP PROGRESSING
DAVE DUNCAN

gentle, then she gets all gnarly. But she put it right into place. But the element of surprise was gone and she still had to do my three fingers. I had to sit down, and she put her foot on my shoulder and it was really wild and she got it all done with no painkillers and grabbed a few pieces of wood [to make a splint] and wrapped it with healing oil and gave me a prayer. I was skating in two weeks; it was the quickest bone heal I've ever had."

IN JULY 1994, TEN MONTHS BEFORE his Slam City takeover, Bob traveled to San Francisco to ride with *Thrasher* editor Phelps and his crew. "I hung with Joey Tershay and Julian [Stranger] and John [Cardiel] and Jake. That was a trippy experience, getting thrown into that. . . . Those guys are 100 percent skateboarders. Twenty-four seven. You *always* have your board, everywhere. That's what impressed me the most. I was like, 'Okay, this is skateboarding.' I finally got a taste of what it was to live the lifestyle. I couldn't believe the motivation. They wanted to find pools and pipes and new terrain. That whole 'trespass, jump in the backyard, skate the pool, and get out' didn't exist in Brazil. They lived skateboarding. It was a big influence on my approach, the perfect influence cuz it was at a time when you'd see skating on TV more often, and it was getting cheesy."

Phelps remembers: "Yeah, he came up to San Francisco and rode with the boys pretty hard. We took him on the road—took him hellriding. We took him to Burnside [Portland's legendary skatepark], and everybody was like, 'Hey, wait a minute, who's that guy?'"

To know Bob now, one wouldn't place him on the crow's nest at Burnside, sucking down his second warm forty-ouncer of Olde English 800 before staggering off to one of Portland's numerous titty bars with a wad of singles for the one-legged stripper. Indeed, Bob's way of life shines in sharp contrast to the stereotypical dirtbag skateboarder swirling the drain in a dubious race to become society's lowest common denominator. "At one point," he explains, "I had a little bit of an identity crisis with the rest of the skateboard community. Then I realized that it was the stereotype that was pressuring me into the identity crisis. Skateboarding is skateboarding: You jump on a skateboard, you go. But the human being is a human being, and we've all got different personalities. And we all skate for different reasons. I take skateboarding as

sacred. And I skate as a form of prayer. I don't like cussing when I'm not making tricks. I try not to get mad and throw my board. To me, that's disrespect to the art, to skateboarding. I've learned to be confident with myself, and it really is kinda fun to be different. I get to change things and influence people.

"Skateboarding gives me a name and fame, and when you have that, people tend to listen to you," he continues. "You inspire people, you get people going, you motivate them just by being yourself. I see it with other skaters, too. When I see Rune [Glifberg], Bucky [Lasek], Tony [Hawk], Jamie Thomas—the guys that are just hucking themselves and going for it—I'm like, 'Man, I can't believe he did that.' And you're like, 'Man, that's insane,' and you get motivated. So in that sense there's a mission there for everybody that's a public figure, people others look up to or listen to. You have a mission. When people ask you what your opinion is on the war or this or that, the usual response is to exclude yourself, to go, 'Oh, I don't know, I'm just a skateboarder. I just skate,' when your answer should be exactly how you feel about those things. . . . I feel like a role model. I asked for it before I was born. You gotta learn to live with that. And in the beginning, I remember saying, 'I just want to skate; I don't really care about this or that.' Then I started realizing that if I want to keep skating and making a living—especially after [my daughter] Lotus was born, that was one of the main things—I can actually balance this. I can be a businessman and a skateboarder. When I'm on the ramp, I shut everything off. But when I'm off the ramp, hey, that's another story. I love the business end of it. Getting things done. The interviews, the travels, the demos, and thousands of people stoked that you're there. Yeah, I'm ready for that.

"The problem with skateboarding is that it's a very physical thing, and we tend to be young and we get really good and become professionals at a really young age, and we're not ready to take on the word *professional* yet. Ability-wise, we might have it, but we're not ready

for it. That's where a lot of problems lie with the kids losing it: they become pro; they get a board; they get a check; they get a lot of money; they start drinking; they start just hanging out, doing dumb stuff, and they think that that's life. Then they blow their money away and they're wrecking their body. Then all of a sudden, they snap their knee and they've blown all their money, they're not number one anymore. They've lost it, they're gone, and there's another guy coming up. The cycle begins again."

Bob's best advice on mixing the two seemingly incongruous worlds of savvy business and pure skateboarding: "You can't do it all yourself. You can't carry all the weight. You need to be confident and know how to deal with people. Communicate. It's all about partnerships."

The partnership he's proudest of connects him to top woman skateboarder Jennifer O'Brien, his gal of several years and the mother of their little girl, born in the spring of 2000. They live in Vista, California, inland a few miles from the northern coast of San Diego County, in a Mediterranean spread with tile floors that's filled with books, art, and photography. Bob's wrap of Roland drums and percussion instruments covers a corner of the main room near the fireplace. His mom has her own flat out back, and between the two-acre produce farm—its products marketed through Burnquist Organics—and the main

UPPING THE ANTE, MARK "RED" SCOTT LOOPS THE FUNNELING PIPE IN REEDSPORT, OREGON. RED, WHO HAD NEVER EVEN SKATED THE PARK BEFORE, PSYCHED HIMSELF UP FOR A GOOD HALF HOUR, STARING AT THE PIPE AND TAKING THE EDGE OFF WITH A FEW BEERS. "IT WAS ONE OF THE SCARIEST THINGS I'VE EVER DONE," HE REMEMBERS. "BEFORE YOU EVEN TRY IT, YOU START THINKING ABOUT HOW YOU VALUE YOUR LIFE. BUT ONCE YOU MAKE IT OVER PAST TWELVE O' CLOCK WITHOUT SLAMMING ON YOUR BACK THEN YOU KNOW YOU GOT IT. UNLESS YOU PUSS OUT." SEPTEMBER 30, 2003
VIDEO: TAVITA SCANLAN

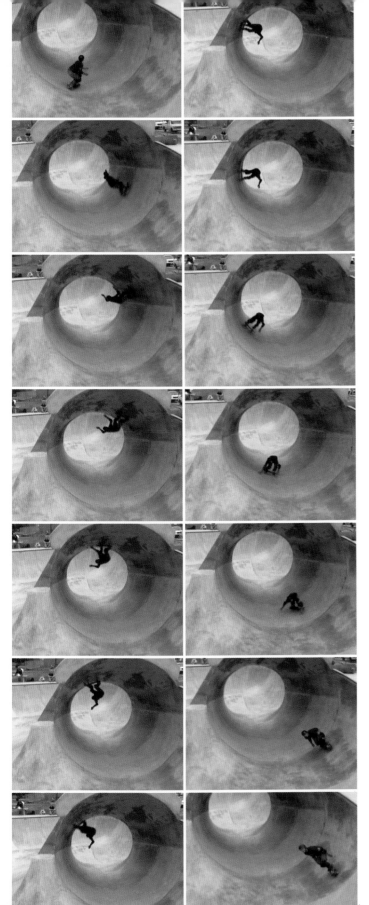

RED IS PROBABLY, POUND FOR POUND, THE GNARLIEST SKATER EVER, BECAUSE HE'S SO MESSY AND HE'S SO POWERFUL. HE DOESN'T GIVE A FUCK. RED RULES. BUT BOB IS JUST LIKE A TERMINATOR, AND HE DOESN'T STOP UNTIL HE BEATS IT OR HE CAN'T WALK

JAKE PHELPS

house are his offices, where he stashes stacks of skateboards he's ridden over the years, shrinkwraps his old casts, and sells equipment and pitches inspiration (in English and Portuguese) via bobburnquist.com, which features links to the Ruckus Society, Act for Change, Natural Resources Defense Council, Free Speech TV, and Worldlink TV. The Web site's homepage ticker reads: "God bless everyone and everything! Have you skated today? Feel like no one understands you? Go skating and take a few slams. Skateboarding saves lives."

ON SATURDAY, DECEMBER 14, 2002, Bob and O'Brien pulled themselves from bed around 7 A.M. and drove to San Bernardino County. Arriving at the planned rendezvous, the EZ Out Burger off Mountain Avenue, they hooked up with legends Lance Mountain and Steve "Salba" Alba. Salba's oldest son, Jesse, nine, was there, too, as was photographer Jon Humphries and videographer Anthony Claravall. After breakfast burritos, the group made for the mountains. Driving into the foothills fanning down from Mount Baldy, they parked down a road in a residential neighborhood. Gathering their gear and leaving the sidewalk and pavement behind, they slipped through a fence posted with "No Trespassing" signs and queued up along a dirt trail. The morning was gray with overcast and dew.

After a bit of a trek, they dropped into a broad concrete spillway snaking down from the mountain. Hiking up the spillway, they at last turned a corner to see a concrete pipe, fourteen-and-a-half feet in diameter, opening from the side of Mount Baldy. A ten-foot-deep pit, as wide as the spillway and bookended by towering vertical walls, gaped between them and the mouth of the pipe. One by one, they filed across a sturdy board spanning the chasm.

Bob, Salba, O'Brien, and Jesse Alba padded up and took some warm-up runs. Salba, who's been riding the Baldy pipe for more than twenty years, drew sweeping arcs across long reaches of the side walls where they sloped up over vertical toward the ceiling. Near the mouth of the pipe, his wheels screeched through tighter turns as the howling echoes in his wake reverberated up and down the pipe. Bob, however, set out with a different approach, starting his run from the back of the pipe, about two hundred yards in from the mouth, and racing for the light at the end of the tunnel with low, long carves at breakneck speed, Bad Brains cranking from his iPod. At the pipe mouth, he eased to a stop and walked slowly back to his starting point, pausing to inspect rough sections and, his mind in deep rehearsal, to stand with his body positioned at different angles while he stared straight up at the ceiling of the pipe, the apex point that a pipe skater calls twelve o'clock.

Claravall set up his video camera while Lance brandished another. Humphries opened his camera bag, set up remote-control flashes, and metered the low light about thirty feet inside the pipe. O'Brien and Salba chatted idly near the mouth of the pipe, comparing conspiracy theories on aliens and the truth and lies of 9/11.

Bob hadn't been to Baldy in a few years and had forgotten how pitted its surface had become, the rough spots nearly rattling him off his board as he practiced his approach. Discouraged but not dissuaded, he borrowed a set of softer wheels from Salba's son, fitted them with his own bearings, and took a few more test runs—much smoother through the rough stuff, certainly, but slower across the smooth sections. Clearly, Bob thought, speed was going to be an issue. Perhaps another wave of doubt rippled through the back of Bob's brain when his iPod seized up, instant silence replacing the adrenaline-inducing Rasta-punk power chords of one of the planet's finest hardcore bands. Bob was bummed. The morning didn't seem to be unfolding in his favor. Fortunately, Claravall's iPod was stocked with some Bad Brains, and he offered up his tunes. A few minutes later, Bob was back on board, making his way to the pipe's deep interior.

Then, suddenly, Bob apparently slipped into a profound insanity, some realm beyond the already crazed disposition of the average—even above-average—skateboarder, because what happened next will forever be described in the legends of skateboarding as one of the craziest stunts ever attempted.

Bob didn't announce from the back of the pipe, "Okay, here I come! I'm gonna try it!" He just went for it. Retracing his practiced line, he scorched toward the mouth of the pipe. About thirty feet from the light of day, during a long frontside turn up where the curve of the pipe met vertical, or nine o'clock, Bob cranked a hard left and sped toward the far wall as head-on as possible. It was the line he'd been practicing, and this time he drew it flawlessly. But instead of cutting it short, as he had done during his warm-up runs, Bob committed fully, pumping with his legs as he climbed the opposite wall. In an instant, he was on the ceiling, completely upside down and focused on riding entirely around the inside of the pipe. Nobody had ever "looped" Baldy, or any other full-pipe, for that matter, and Bob was out to be the first. And he was looking good for that split second between nine and twelve o'clock.

I JUST WANT TO DO THINGS THAT HAVEN'T BEEN DONE BEFORE. I'M OPEN TO SKATEBOARD ANYTHING AND EVERYTHING, WHATEVER. WE'LL BE ON A TRIP—I CAN STREET SKATE. IF WE FIND A POOL, I'LL SKATE A POOL. IF WE FIND A LOOP, I'LL LOOP IT. IF WE FIND A PIPE, I'LL RIDE IT. IF THERE'S A LONG-JUMP, WE'LL JUMP IT. THAT'S WHAT I WANT TO DO. I WANT TO BE ABLE TO SKATE IT ALL. AND NOT JUST SCRATCH IT. I MEAN ACTUALLY SKATE IT GOOD

BOB BURNQUIST

BOB BURNQUIST'S UNPRECEDENTED LOOP ATTEMPT
(LEFT) AT MOUNT BALDY UNSETTLED THE SKATEBOARD WORLD BOTH FOR ITS SHEER INSANITY
AND BECAUSE *TRANSWORLD SKATEBOARDING* MAGAZINE BROKE AN UNWRITTEN RULE BY
PUTTING IT ON THE COVER EVEN THOUGH HE DIDN'T PULL IT OFF (RIGHT). DECEMBER 14, 2002
PHOTOS: JON HUMPHRIES

BOB IS ONE OF THE RADDEST EVER. . . . PETER HEWITT IS THE RADDEST IN MY BOOK IN TODAY'S SKATING. HEWITT IS THE DUANE PETERS OF THE 2000S. AND BOB IS THE STEVE CABALLERO OR EDDIE ELGUERA OF TODAY, BUT GNARLIER

SALBA

Then something truly frightening happened.

Bob's weight was too far toward the tail of his board. And at the top of his heels-over-head carve around rugged Baldy, as his woman and friends sucked in their breath, half astonished, half terrified by this unprecedented attempt at upside-down skateboarding, Bob wilsoned.

Wilsoning on flat ground is bad enough, and any skateboarder should consider himself let off easy if he merely limps away with a bruised tailbone. But an upside-down wilson? Fourteen feet above rutted concrete?

Doomed, Bob fell headfirst toward the floor, his board zinging away, his helmet really not much of a cushion against a direct fall on the head. Halfway through his free fall, however, Bob's life was saved by a miraculous mix of feline reflexes, survival instinct, surely some higher power, and a bit of good luck. He spun a quick, clean backflip and landed squarely on his feet at the bottom of the pipe.

Lance nearly had a heart attack. Salba 'bout shit his shorts. The others shook their heads and stared and blinked and gulped with what could be described only as utter disbelief. Bob just grabbed his board—the look on his face saying, "Oh, I *got* that"—and skated to the back of the pipe to try it again.

Lance's memory: "We were filming cuz we know Bob; he was saying he was gonna try it, so you better be rolling. My footage is just ridiculous: he's not even in frame or nothing. I panicked so hard when he tried it. His first one was gnarly. I've had a gun pulled on me before and I thought I was gonna get shot, and it was exactly the same feeling. Your heart's out of control and you're like jittery. It was so gnarly. We were just, 'Oh, my . . . you gotta be kidding. Did we just see that?' It was crazy."

And Jon's: "It was definitely the most insane thing I've seen. I was freaking out for sure, but I think I would have been freaking out more if I had been Salba and had been going there for all those years. Salba just freaked. That was the best thing: just watching Salba's reaction."

"The whole time," Anthony remembers, "me and Lance and Jon were like, I mean, I didn't even know if it was really going to happen. I couldn't even imagine how it could happen. It went from not even being able to get my head around it—you know, talking to Salba and he's been skating it for like twenty years and people have been talking about looping it for that long and no one's even ever really tried it—and now we're here, and it's not the right equipment, wrong wheels, and it feels really rushed. It went from that feeling, the feeling that it's not the day—then all of a sudden Bob's upside down."

Half a dozen tries and as many harrowing falls later, Bob had pumped cleanly through twelve o'clock and was coming back down, feet on his board, mind etched with determination. He made it all the way over to nine o'clock on the far wall, the expression on his face screaming, "I got it! I got it!" but his body tipped wrong and his feet drifted and he slipped out. By this point, his spectators—who now included two random kids who came to skate but settled in for the show—were starting to believe the impossible. Lance and Salba looked at each other like, "Whoa, this *is* possible, and we're gonna see it *right now*."

But a few tries later, Bob went down, slamming so hard it was tough to tell if he'd get up without a stretcher. But he did. And tried it again. Then another bone-stressing slam. And another. Then, on his fourteenth attempt, Bob fell from the ceiling yet again, his spinning free fall sending him in an awkward direction. He landed on his feet on the curve of the wall and buckled like a dropped prizefighter, the sheer pressure of impact splitting the third metacarpal in his right foot and spraining his left ankle.

Down for the count.

"And I was just coming out of knee surgery," Bob remembers, "so I was already kinda feeling that. Everything was tweaking. I remember my wrist was hurting. I was supposed to crawl out of there, but I couldn't put my hand down and I couldn't put my knee down and I couldn't really stand, so basically it was like, sit on my board and have people help me out of there.

"Baldy was make it or break it, and I broke it. But it could've been a lot worse."

I DON'T PUT ANYTHING PAST BOB

JON HUMPHRIES

AT 4:20 IN THE AFTERNOON OF NOVEMBER 23, 2003, BOB
CLOSED THE CHAPTER ON UPSIDE-DOWN
SKATEBOARDING BY SUCCESSFULLY LOOPING A
"NATURAL" FULL-PIPE
(ONE NOT MADE FOR SKATEBOARDING).
THE STEEL CONDUIT, THIRTY-TWO FEET LONG AND
TWELVE FEET IN DIAMETER, WAS A PROP IN A
UPS COMMERCIAL FEATURING BOB'S PARTNER JEN O'BRIEN, WHO TALKED THE SHIPPING COMPANY INTO GIVING IT TO
HER AFTER THE SHOOT. BOB AND JEN HAD IT TRUCKED HOME, WHERE IT'S
PART OF THEIR MASSIVE SKATE COMPOUND

PHOTO: MICHAEL O'MEALLY

11

SKATEPARKS

(HELLPOUR)

DUSTY, GREASY, AND SPRINKLED WITH QUICKLY CURING CONCRETE SPLATTER.

MARK "RED" SCOTT CARVED BACKSIDE AT BREAKNECK SPEED THROUGH THE THIRTEEN-FOOT-DEEP CAPSULE

CORNER OF THE LATEST MASTERPIECE SCULPTED BY DREAMLAND SKATEPARKS.

Drawing his line down the adjoining flat wall, Red straightened his legs at the bottom of his turn, pumping still more speed from the lower reaches of ten-foot transitions before racing across the flat and up the opposite wall. Under a red Independent ballcap and concrete-frosted sunglasses, Red's expression was both an ear-to-ear grin brought on by the smooth, almost frighteningly fast lines offered by this virgin Dreamland bowl and a crooked snarl aimed at the daunting seven-foot hip he had been trying to launch over all afternoon.

One more flat-wall carve placed him before and below that hip with what seemed to be enough speed to click from its pipe-lined lip, snag his board backside near the apex of a four-foot-high, ten-foot-long aerial, turn and dive for smooth reentry, and ride away toward the next wall. But what happened next had happened before. Not quite enough speed. Red was going to come up short, and he knew it. Just before touchdown, he kicked away his board and prepared for impact. He hit the concrete feet first and took a few stutter steps before lunging forward into a succession of bone-bruising rolls during which, somehow, his left index finger stopped while the rest of his five-foot-ten, two-hundred-pound body kept on going. His doomed digit stretched a bit and bent back, ripping apart the skin where it joined his palm. Tumbling to a stop in the bottom of the bowl, the ass of his Carhartt pants ripped open, Red retrieved his wayward board and climbed to the deck alongside his Dreamland crew members. His mind lost in a rehash of that last attempt, he didn't notice the blood pouring from the wide, deep gash in his hand.

"Hey, Mark," called out Sage Bolyard to his longtime friend and coworker, "yer bleedin'."

"Oh," Red replied, calmly inspecting his torn finger, blood streaming across his palm.

"Looks like that might need some stitches," Sage said through the gap in the side of his smile—one tooth lost to an errant baseball, the other to hard candy—then dropped into his own backside capsule-corner carve, wrapping it around toward the opposing flat wall and up into an invert on coping.

PREVIOUS:
RICK THE BUM, BURNSIDE, 1993
PHOTO: KENT DAHLGREN

Red wiped the blood on his pants and took a quick breather as Jimmy "the Greek" Marcus frontside-grinded the park's tallest wall, a Dreamland monster checking in at fourteen feet, the top four of it pure vertical. No time for stitches, Red wiped his palm again against his grimy Carhartts and tailed his board toward the bowl's edge as New York–based filmmakers Rick Charnoski and Coan "Buddy" Nichols, gathering footage for their 2003 film *Northwest*, pointed Super-8 cameras at Dave "Shaggy" Palmer until he bailed on a fakie ollie. The coast clear, Red dropped in, his expression now more snarl than grin, blood still pumping from his wounded meat hook, and retraced his line. But this time he stuck that backside air over the hip, capping off a hellacious work week with hoots from his friends, a little blood on the ground, and the inaugural session at one of the world's most daunting skateboard parks.

IT WAS A GOLDEN DAY indeed—a work-free Saturday in August 2002, in fact, with Rocky Mountain skies and an easy breeze funneling through the Magic Valley—for the Dreamland crew and their friends and anybody else in Hailey, Idaho, who had been watching this park come together, pour by pour.

A few days earlier, classic rock blasting from KIKX FM, the Dreamland crew had applied the final trowel-swipes to the only skatepark full-pipe built west of the Mississippi in nearly a quarter century, since skateboarding's initial '70s skatepark era. Fifteen feet in diameter and twenty-four feet long, the concrete tube was also a first for the Dreamland crew, something they'd dreamed of during their four years together but had had to wait for the right time, place, and budget to build. It was worth the wait. In Hailey, everything fell into place. Off the bat, the townspeople in charge of the skatepark budget had graced Dreamland with a completely clean slate, promising not to meddle with whatever design Red and his crew dreamed up. Also, after

> # I JUST FIGURED THAT BUILDING MY OWN SHIT UNDER THE BRIDGE WOULD BE FASTER THAN GOING TO CITY COUNCIL MEETINGS AND ASKING FOR A SKATEPARK. DURING MY WHOLE YOUNG SKATING DAYS, I WAS NEVER ABLE TO SKATE ONE SPOT FOR MORE THAN FIVE MINUTES WITHOUT GETTING KICKED OUT, SO MY WHOLE ATTITUDE WAS "FUCK YOU"
> BRET TAYLOR

nearly four years of fundraising, the nonprofit Hailey Skateboard Park, Inc., headed by Andy Andrews, carrying a bright torch for his dead son, Tyler, who had long lobbied for a local skatepark, had banked a cool quarter million. Last, the Dreamland crew was in pretty good form. True, original crew member Jeff Kimbrough was back in Lincoln City, Oregon, for the birth of his second child, a little girl named Hunter, while veterans Mark "Marty" Hubbard and Stefan Hauser had both recently departed Dreamland to launch their own park-building companies. But Red, Sage, Mike Swim, and Tavita Scanlan had worked long and hard together, achieving a flowing synchronicity and needing very little verbal communication. Their process perfected, they knew who was best at what—be it forming, barring, shooting, floating, edging, or finishing—and they

had a few volunteers and low-end laborers to boss around and clean equipment at day's end. Plus, just for the pipe-pouring week, Dreamland had recruited Bob "Secret Weapon" Kotas, a longtime friend of Swim's with a résumé in carpentry and masonry.

Building off the pipe's bottom half (sculpted a month earlier with two easy pours), the crew spent the early days of the week framing up the top half of the looming structure, supporting its arching ceiling with a heavily cross-braced redundancy of stabilizing four-by-fours and two-by-sixes and crisscrossing it with hundreds of sticks of three- and four-gauge reinforcement bar. When it came time to pour, they pounded together an OSHA-nightmare matrix of rickety scaf-folds, tied off the concrete hose with thick rope, and hoisted it to the top of the pipe—nearly twenty feet above ground zero—where much of the mud would be sprayed against the Masonite forms. In a week's time, these smooth forms would be stripped away, leaving a baby-butt-smooth riding surface inside the pipe.

The whole operation went off without a hitch until menacing clouds threatened from the north. Twenty minutes later, during a critical phase of the pour, as Scanlan and Red balanced on the apex, pumping

FOR THE MOST PART, CITY BUREAUCRATS DON'T HAVE A CLUE ABOUT SKATEPARKS. SKATEBOARDING DIDN'T EXIST FOR THEM. THEY'RE GRASPING AT AIR THAT THEY DON'T EVEN KNOW HOW TO BREATHE

STEFAN HAUSER

pound after pound of wet concrete against an already floated yet still quivering section that threatened to mudslide away at the slightest nudge, the sky opened and it started to hail. Hard.

Red yelled to his crew over the hail's machine-gun rattle: "Let's stop for a second, get some rain gear and some tarps, and finish her off!" Everybody scrambled, donned their slickers, tied off a tarp to protect the fresh pour from the surface-pitting ice pellets, and finished her off. "It was a candy bar," Sage would later claim, downplaying the day, while Red says, "I was kinda sketched on the whole deal, up there shooting mud, the whole time thinking, 'More weight, more weight.'" But the forms held, and the result, true to Dreamland's part-genius, part-mad-scientist design reputation, was a full-pipe one could skateboard through *and* over. It was a gigantic hollow speed bump rising from the center of the park. The biggest speed bump on the planet. Nothing like it had ever been built.

So, naturally, the week came to a close with the Dreamland crew stinking up the inside of Red's job-site trailer—a stretch fifth wheel with gold-glittered wood paneling and plush orange shag—while slamming through a few half-racks of Pabst Blue Ribbon, a lot of which got spilled with each can-clashing toast. Well into their second half-rack, Red and Sage squared off with power tools—Red and his trusty Stihl chainsaw versus Sage and a water-cooled blade designed to cut concrete—but instead of laying into each other (as drunk old friends often should), they hacked apart beer cans and large scraps of plywood, filling the trailer with sawdust and shrapnel.

If they didn't cut loose every so often, concrete work would surely turn them old real quick. There's nothing easy about it. After days of displacing massive volumes of dirt and rock with excavators, Hailey's big bowl, for example, was shaped up with a Bobcat, shovels, and a steamroller and hand-pushed compactor. Forms were cut from plywood and two-by-fours and staked down with sledgehammers. Long, heavy lengths of three-inch pipe coping were welded into place as the entire pool was laced with unwieldy twenty-foot lengths of rebar, scalding all day in the summer sun. (If a bowl is to be blessed with pool coping, the heavy blocks are set as final touches, one by one, seams packed with wet concrete and then troweled smooth.) Then the truckloads of mud arrived, usually around 7 A.M. Before their aching joints had even been warmed by Texaco coffee, the crew fired up the Putzmeister hopper and a LeRoy air compressor, which provided the surging, two-hundred-psi lifeblood of their shotcrete operation. At least two strong men would position the mud-filled rubber hose, its nozzle spattering a fine mist and emitting a deafening hiss that nearly drowned out the nozzleman's commands—"Two!" for on, "One!" for off—to whoever was manning the flow-control switch. "Two up, motherfucker, two up!" was Sage's typical holler as he heaved the heavy hose across one shoulder and pointed the nozzle at a skeleton of

SLAYER AT FORTY-FIVE RPM IS EXCEPTIONAL. IT ENABLED US TO RUN AROUND AND THROW BEER BOTTLES OUT THE WINDOW
KENT DAHLGREN

rebar and wood forms soon to disappear under tons of wet concrete. "One! One! One!" he'd scream as the mud piled a hair past grade and Red and the rest waded in with rakes, screed boards, and floats custom-built with crescent curves to match the slope of the wall. After it was floated, they swiped at it with magnesium trowels before polishing it off with finish trowels, working on their knees, shouldering with long arcs into the hardening 'crete until it simply could not be worked any longer, always racing the clock as the water reacted with the cement to bond the rock and sand. Once concrete is kicked, that's it. There's nothing more that can be done to smooth its surface, aside from obliterating it with a jackhammer and starting over, which, in the creed of any self-respecting concrete crew, should never happen.

Concrete work is hard, heavy labor from start to finish, and it takes its bodily toll in kinked back, neck, shoulder, and forearm muscles; in clattering lungs stuccoed with cement dust; and in throbbing, swollen burns that blister up when concrete splatter cures on exposed flesh, sucking moisture from the skin. Red even sports deep fire scars across his left arm, relics from his formative years as a self-taught skatepark sculptor underneath the damp and dirty eastern end of Portland, Oregon's Burnside Bridge.

THE EVENT THAT QUIETLY HELPED to resurrect skateboarding from its third slump and that paved the way for the greatest skatepark revolution occurred under a cloak of darkness in the late summer or early fall of 1990. Past the witching hour on a cold night, Bret Taylor, then twenty, threw a five-gallon bucket, a shovel, a wheelbarrow, a few bags of cement, and what was left of the beer into the back of his '71 Toyota Land Cruiser. He yarded up his roommates Osage Buffalo

RED HOISTS AN ANDRECHT PLANT IN THE
BIG BOWL, SUMMER 1991
PHOTO: KENT DAHLGREN

and Chuck Willis and drove from their beat-up rental, just off southeast Portland's Martin Luther King Jr. Boulevard, to the sour underbelly of the Burnside Bridge, where fall-down drunks and dirt-cheap hookers vied for dry shelter.

The Burnside Bridge underside had also long been a fairly popular hangout for Portland skateboarders, a dry piece of asphalt in a city pelted by eight months of rain each year. It also served as a somewhat safe zone from Portland cops, who in truth were more likely to bust the illicit debauchery of the prevailing blow-jobs-for-crack economy than to brandish their ticket books at bored skateboarders. But, best of all, this forgotten and shoved-aside dry slice of the city featured a massive wall, slanting from the rough asphalt at eighty degrees to a towering height. This wall was skateable. Across the pitted and cracked asphalt, skateboarders pushed mightily toward the banked wall. At the juncture, they lifted their front wheels to meet the angled surface and just bashed up the looming slab as high as their speed and talent would carry them. Powering a few feet up, turning, and riding back down to the flat was an impressive rush but still seemed like kid stuff in light of the wall's sheer overhead yardage.

Then Bret arrived with his tattered bags of cement. Skateboarding would never be the same.

Bret and his buddies, already good and buzzed, pulled under the bridge and unloaded his Land Cruiser. They gathered ingredients: Osage wandered off toward the river with the five-gallon bucket and returned with it half full; Bret and Chuck scooped gravel and dirt from an empty lot nearby; everybody gathered trash and piled it against the wall; and somebody split open the sacks of cement. Mixing the concoction with the shovel, they scooped the wet concrete onto the trash pile filling the juncture between the asphalt and the wall, mellowing out its harsh angle. Their crude addition was just a lump, really, a couple feet high and a foot again wide, that somewhat smoothed the truck-breaking transition between

ground zero and the slanted monolith. When it cured, their lump certainly wasn't a monument of concrete craftsmanship, but it definitely made the below-bridge scene a more appealing place to ride, enabling the brave to climb higher up that mountain of a wall.

Red wasn't there that fateful night, and when he learned that something had been built without his help, he was quietly annoyed. But his cold mood would be quickly erased with one ride up the new hit. Very soon, however, reaching previously unattainable altitudes on the wall wasn't enough. They had tasted the sky, and within a week's time, it was inevitable that they would need something more to quench their thirst for speed and altitude and weightless thrill. So Red, his greasy hair sweat-staining the collar of his duct-tape-patched '70s down ski vest, built a second bank, a bit bigger than the first and with some curve to it, about ten feet to one side of Bret's lump. Now there were two hits, a pair of skateable bank-to-walls tucked away under a dry roof in a section of town too shitty to get kicked out of. The spot's best line carried skaters up one bank and down the other, bridging the broad gap between them, where, on a good day, junkie bums passed out in their own piss, curled up on a wretched sofa. On better days, Red and the rest took turns on Jay Graham's motorcycle, speeding each other toward the wall on a towline, then letting loose like a hellion-loaded slingshot.

The crisp fall fell to another bitter Portland winter. Subzero wind chill swept off the Willamette River as freezing rain drove in sideways under the bridge, leaving dirty puddles in which the skateboarders mixed small batches of concrete, smoothing out freshly built banks with tails from snapped skateboards. Amid the dirt and vermin and pigeon shit, a handful of banks

JEFF GROSSO AT KELLY BELMAR'S HOMEMADE BACKYARD BOWL, HUNTINGTON BEACH, CALIFORNIA, WHERE MASON RICK CARJE CUT HIS TEETH BEFORE FOUNDING RCMC, A SKATEPARK-BUILDING COMPANY THAT BUILT ALL THE VANS PARKS. JANUARY 1999
PHOTO: RHINO

BURNSIDE'S ALWAYS BEEN THE SPOT WHERE I FELT SAFE. WHENEVER BAD SHIT WENT DOWN—IF THEIR FOLKS WERE OUT ON THEM, OR IF A GIRLFRIEND OR BOYFRIEND DUMPED THEM, OR THEY GOT BEAT UP BY A BUNCH OF JOCKS OR GANGSTERS, OR THEIR LANDLORD THREW THEM OUT, OR WHATEVER— BURNSIDE IS WHERE PEOPLE WOULD GO
TANYA GOLDEN

went up against the big wall, followed by a waist-high turnaround quarter-pipe formed up with mounds of garbage. Red's memory: "It was a bank to kink to bricks to a curb on top. It was kill. A lot of that early shit had a lot of style and character cuz it was so ghetto." And none of it, by any standard, was easy to skate. A beer-buzzed take-off across rough asphalt and pigeon crap to a kinked wall-ride in thirty-degree daytime highs doesn't exactly make for a skateboarder's dream spot. But it was skateboarding at its best. In a town full of kids, teenagers, and young adults who had, with zero results, long called on their government to provide them a legal place to ride, the renegade skateboard park beneath the Burnside Bridge represented

An illustration/graphic separator

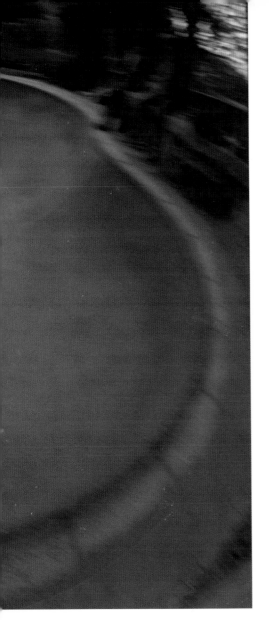

nothing less than a gutsy, unglorified drive by a handful of disenfranchised skateboarders to build a scene in a city politically and climatically inhospitable to their way of life.

By the time city officials caught wind of the clandestinely growing concrete curves beneath the Burnside Bridge, Red had completely taken over Bret's original inspiration and, through his visionary motivation and raging workaholic benders, shaped the project as his own. Bret was irritated, to be sure, but didn't let it bother him, as long as something was getting built and the area was kept clean.

It was the skateboarders' proud self-sufficiency and outright respect for their precarious fortuity that most impressed Joanne Ferrero, who owned a car-part distribution business next door to what had been dubbed the Burnside Project. From her fourth-floor office window she watched the young skaters jump off their boards and rush roadside to flag down a Ross

ME AND HUBBARD USED TO SIT IN HIS BASEMENT AND DREAM ABOUT BUILDING SKATEPARKS. YOU KNOW, "YEAH, SOMEDAY WE'LL TRAVEL THE WORLD BUILDING PARKS." AND NOW WE KINDA ARE

MIKE SWIM

Island concrete truck heading home from a pour, begging the driver to dump off surplus mud, maybe a half yard, whatever he had. She watched them clean up garbage and paint over graffiti and run off the junkies and whores. And when it at last came time for Red to spit out the plug of Copenhagen tobacco behind his lower lip and rally his troops to tell the city's elected officials exactly what a bunch of unsupervised hell-raisers were up to on this city-owned right-of-way, Joanne went to bat for Burnside.

The most lucid memories of the history of Burnside always contain an ancient dictum: the right people came together at the right time. Along with the skaters themselves, Joanne, certainly, was one of the right people, nothing less than the "godmother of Burnside," according to Red. Joanne's tireless support drew tolerance from surrounding business owners, not all of them readily convinced that the park shouldn't be leveled into a parking lot. Her enthusiasm was matched by that of Linda Dobson, an aide to City Commissioner Mike Lindberg, who oversaw the Parks Bureau. At the peak of the political pyramid sat sympathetic Mayor Bud Clarke, one of the most popular and progressive of Portland's leaders, whose son, Nick Clarke, skated Burnside regularly and had helped out on a few pours. Police officer John Larkin's testimony concurs with Joanne's, adding, "It's the first time skateboarders have waved at me with all five fingers."

By the summer of 1992 Portland politicos had passed a resolution stating their support of "the community's desire to continue the skateboarding under the east end of the Burnside bridge," as long as the skaters kept

I DON'T BUILD SKATEPARKS FOR SAFETY. THEY'RE NOT BUILT TO BE SAFE. IT'S NOT A PLAYGROUND, IT'S A SKATEPARK. YOU CAN'T EXPECT TO DROP YOUR KID OFF EVERY DAY AND EXPECT HIM TO COME HOME WALKING

MARK "MARTY" HUBBARD

policing themselves "to assure continued good neighbor relations with the surrounding businesses and community as a whole." It also set in stone a fear that had haunted Burnside skaters since day one: "Skateboarders recognize that their use of the site may be terminated at any time." Yet the agreement, dubbed a peace pact by then-*Oregonian* columnist Osker Spicer, both explicitly and implicitly empowered the skaters to maintain and expand their own skatepark as long as they remained tactful neighbors.

These first few years were the hardest for the Burnside locals. Not only were city officials and police officers poised to pull the park's plug at the slightest provocation, the skaters had only their own marginal savings from which to scrape together money for cement. Then, piling insult on top of their impover-

ishment, a dangling carrot rotted away. A long-available forty-one-thousand-dollar park-levy cache had seemed destined to find a home as the skaters' years-old demand for a public park was at last heard by receptive public officials. Burnside builders figured a chunk of that change could be put toward concrete and tools, plus construction of at least one other free, permanent park elsewhere within city limits. But they got none of that. Howard Weiner, owner of Cal Skate skate shop, secured the windfall and opened City Skate, an indoor, pay-to-ride park of wooden ramps, complete with a Cal Skate pro shop. Sage's rage: "That money should have gone into a free, concrete park. And then Howard hired a Canadian crew to build it when he knew we were all builders. That's bullshit." City Skate folded within two years. From the perspec-

tive of Burnside's original locals, Weiner losing his shirt on the venture was poetic street justice. Adding insult to Weiner's financial injury, those same locals often broke into City Skate after it closed, skating long into the night for free.

All the while, Red and the rest kept at it down under the bridge, scrounging cement money, mixing batches by hand. A decade later, Red would enjoy the relative luxury of hollowing out a Dreamland park with

WE BUILT OUR OWN WORLD IN THE DEAD CENTER OF THE CITY. WE KICKED THE HOOKERS ON DOWN THE ROAD, WE BEAT THE JUNKIES ON DOWN THE ROAD, AND THE CITY PEOPLE SAW THAT WE WEREN'T JUST A BUNCH OF SHITBAG SKATERS

SAGE BOLYARD

headless pigeons from the rafters as warnings to the rest; Chuck Willis secretly sipping Hamm's beer from a Coke can while other locals, all spitfire and pride, tore into California crews that forgot to check their cool-guy attitudes at the border; Coy "Germ" Hill living in festering squalor for many moons inside Burnside's damp, cramped tool shack, which reeked like death on a bad day; and Red himself, no stranger to Burnside's shit-yer-pants-drunk tradition of cheap-beer benders and amnesiac hangovers, bouncing his head at high speed against one of the bridge's vertical pillars, spinning with fright and vertigo as the swirling psychedelic hallucinations of a massive headache crowded his vision.

These work-hard, play-hard years, this formative era, the first half decade of Burnside's legacy, were summed up by an overhead tag left by some mysterious midnight spraypainter: "Fast Eddy Plays Dirty Rock and Roll."

excavators and bulldozers. The earliest locals, however, crafted Burnside with pickaxes and shovels. Imagine Kent Dahlgren cutting salvaged inch-thick rebar with a dull hacksaw before pounding it into place with a massive hunk of concrete. Or Alex Lilly patching a leak in the big bowl with a handful of cement pressed into place with a discarded heroin spoon he found in the weeds. "And one day Red had this bright idea to pour gasoline on the concrete and light it on fire so it would set up faster," remembers Joanne, "and then I went to visit him in the hospital."

Aside from all the trials by fire and hard-learned lessons as Red and the rest of the locals taught themselves how to form and finish concrete, the skate scene itself, too, had little sympathy for the weak. Picture this: Sage dragging dead, overdosed junkies out of the way so he could ride; Dave McBride catching a near-fatal case of spinal meningitis from slamming an open wound through a pile of pigeon shit and then, after his strength returned, hanging murdered,

BORN ON CHRISTMAS EVE 1970, Red was raised just outside Portland near the small town of Tigard, then mostly farmland. He was a shy kid, pretty good at soccer, but hung up his cleats when it got so competitive it wasn't fun anymore. He enjoyed building tree forts and going down to the creek with his dog, and he was first turned on to skateboarding by his older brother, who spun 360s on a banana board in the '70s. For a while Red rode a generic Nash skateboard, the day's department-store special, and by the time he was thirteen, about when he quit soccer, he was completely hooked. He saved up, bought a Mark "Gator" Rogowski pro model, and broke it in at the few crappy spots around Tigard—the ledges down at the sewage plant, a few slanted walls, numerous painted curbs. One day in 1986, while skating the Tigard Theater Banks, he met Dahlgren, and they'd remain friends for life.

Though his father was a carpenter, Red didn't get one hand of help in building his first half-pipe. Situated next to the family barn, Red's ramp stood six

WASHINGTON STREET BUILDERS AT WORK, 2002
PHOTOS: SARAH HARRON

feet high on one side, nine on the other, with a pitched lip. It wasn't an easy ride; Red often skated alone. The same could be said of his next creation, an eight-foot-high, eight-foot-wide half-pipe, both walls with kinked transitions, which he had drawn freehand with a pencil. He soon widened the ramp to twelve feet, then twenty-four. A foot of vert topped each wall. "Everyone was scared to ride it," he remembers. "So I cut two feet off one side, a foot off the other, just so my friends would come skate. But they still didn't come out, so I said, 'Fuck it,' and put four feet of vert on one side."

His next project had him in Jay Graham's girlfriend's backyard in Portland, nailing together a bowled-off, capsule-shaped ramp until the city threatened to tag it. So Red and his dad hacked it apart with a chainsaw, hauled it back to Tigard, and rigged it to the existing ramp, though some of the seams didn't line up quite right. Still, Red skated it alone a lot, also sessioning a few jump ramps and railroad ties he had scattered

around the family driveway. Eventually, wet weather and a swarm of carpenter ants ate away at his half-pipe, and Red's dad wanted it gone. After one last farewell session, Red and Dahlgren set it on fire and danced around it with their shirts off.

Working steadily since he was twelve, first as a paperboy, later launching his own landscaping business, Red spent all his free time skating, weather permitting.

At sixteen, maintaining a B grade-point average, he was driving south to Eugene every weekend to ride the Cage Ramp, where he met Mark "Marty" Hubbard, who was living in a pantry at Buddy Nichols's house. Hubbard and Red would later become the best of friends and eventually build skateparks together. When Red married in 1999, Hubbard was one of his best men. The other was Sage, whom Red had met one afternoon in the early '90s in Portland's Paranoia Park.

Sage, born in Portland and raised in Olympia, Washington, had moved back to town and was slowly discovering Portland's skate scene. When he and Red spotted each other in Paranoia Park, they became instant skateboard brethren. The first thing they did together was shoulder-tap a bum to buy them beer at Three Brothers Market. Red also took Sage down to the bridge when Burnside was not much more than those first few lumps against the big wall. They soon ended up housemates at the infamous Crust Palace.

Rotting near the corner of Fourteenth and Fremont, the Crust Palace, as Sage remembers, was a two-story shithole whose best features were peeling green paint, a really crummy front porch, and a downstairs bathroom with an old, stained bedsheet for a door. Sage lived upstairs, where the A-frame cut into his bedroom's headspace. Red posted up in the barn out back with his then-girlfriend and mother of his first child, a little girl. Subhuman conditions aside, overhead was dirt-cheap at the Crust Palace. For several years it was home to a handful of actual rent-paying tenants and just as many, sometimes more, transient floppers who passed through town to get gassed on other people's beer, check out punk shows, and skate Burnside. From the Crust Palace's roomy backyard, Red and the rest dug out several cubic yards of dirt and used it for fill at the constantly evolving park. (The excavation left a boot-shaped void, which they later partially lined with concrete. Though they were unable to finish the Crust Bowl before moving out, they did create cherished memories by conning neighborhood squirts to drop in, then laughed their asses off with each inevitable slam.)

By the late '90s, Burnside had earned international

YOU HAVE TO BECOME COMPLETELY INVOLVED, ALWAYS THINKING ABOUT DESIGNS AND DOWN THE LINE AND WHERE YOU'RE GONNA LIVE AND ALWAYS STARTING FROM SCRATCH IN EVERY NEW TOWN. IT BECOMES SO PERSONAL. IT'S YOUR LIFE. I'VE HAD TO MAKE A LOT OF SACRIFICES. IT'S CUT INTO MY MUSIC AND WRITING, BUT YOU HAVE TO BE 100 PERCENT IF YOU'RE ON THE CREW. IT HAS TO BE THAT WAY CUZ THE PARKS DEMAND IT
TAVITA SCANLAN

recognition for its challenging design and cultural mayhem. Out-of-luck, out-of-town skaters migrated to Burnside to build new lives in Portland, couch-surfing with new friends and signing up for Oregon Trail food cards. Many locals and transplants alike have fared well over the years, sending down a root or two and finding direction, friendship, love, and a cleaned-up existence in the subculture—a city of its own—thriving under that bridge. Some, however, have ended up buried under one too many blackouts at the Jolly (a nearby dive more commonly called the Bucket, for its three-dollar thirty-two-ounce "buckets" of beer) and have burned through entire paychecks in single sittings at video poker machines. Others have become very familiar with the inside of a jail cell. Burnside's anniversary parties, thrown each year on Halloween, were something else entirely—for an understated version, think hard skating, hard drinking, hard drugs, and hard rock dressed in a demented costume, and then set it free with fireworks, firearms, and flying feces.

Structurally, the park reached capacity in about 1997: Nearly every available square foot under the high-noon shadow of the eastern reach of Burnside Bridge offered a skateable structure. The big wall, the square bowl, and the kick-out quarter-pipe dominated the east. The northern edge held an eight-foot-tall curved wall with a hip capped with steel coping, plus a pyramid hit leading to a high line straight up and down a three-foot-wide pillar that reached the roof. Hitting the western boundary, along the road, skaters could carve the elbow, grind the curb-lipped quarter-pipe wall, lunge up

a pillar, dive for the big bowl, and take swipes at the crow's nest, an improbably steep corner full of vert and mangled pool coping overlooking a pair of the foulest Honey Bucket latrines known to man. Along the southern edge raced a narrow, pump-bump speed track and a metal-lipped flat wall that curved around to match the big wall's kick-out quarter-pipe. In the middle of the mix ran a spine, a Twinkie-shaped pump bump, and the infamous punk wall, an abrupt tombstone backed up against the deepest reaches of the big bowl.

Burnside has never been an easy place to skate. And for that reason, among others, some skateboarders have chosen not to frequent the place. But skateboarders who over the years have dedicated a fair amount of time and blood to Burnside have found rich reward. Because it offers a spectrum of challenges—from bathtub-tight transitions to gigantic ones, from smooth metal coping to jagged concrete lips, from street-inspired pyramid hits to a yard of solid vert capped with pregnant pool coping, all linked by countless lines—any dedicated local with a natural supply of adrenaline and, perhaps, slightly oversized *huevos* can become an exceptional skateboarder. Simply stated: If a skater can achieve and maintain speed and adaptability in good form at Burnside, he or she can go on to skate anything, anywhere, with outstandingly aggressive grace. For this envelope-pushing influence alone, the world of skateboarding owes a great debt to Burnside and the men who made it.

Burnside's legacy, however, and that of its creators, would not remain confined to the cold shadows of eastern Portland's industrial core.

IN THE FALL OF 1997, JEFF KIMBROUGH was living in Lincoln City, a wet and foggy town on Oregon's coast, southwest of Portland. Between long spells of rain and construction jobs, Kimbrough skated the old L.C. park, a rough and kinked snake run spilling into a five-foot-deep bowl built in the early '90s. By that time, Burnside had long glowed with international recognition, and skatepark fever was spreading. In southern Oregon, Florida-bred Eric Dawkins, with the talented trowel of Mike Swim, was designing and building concrete parks in Jacksonville, Ashland, Talent, and Medford. Inspired, Kimbrough told Lincoln City officials that they should build a modern indoor park so skaters would have a dry and decent spot to ride. Ron Ploger, Lincoln City's parks and recreation director, informed Kimbrough that twenty-eight thousand dollars in urban renewal funds had been set aside to resurface the city's existing park. Kimbrough told Ploger that he knew just the guy to spearhead the remodel, a man, he explained, with both concrete and skateboarding experience.

Kimbrough had never met Red before. Starting his search at Burnside in the middle of winter, he eventually tracked him to an indoor ramp park in Salem. Red was intrigued by Kimbrough's plans, and they soon met again in Portland to improvise a design for a complete rebuild of Lincoln City's park. Months passed. At last they had Ploger's financial green light and a sheet of graph paper covered with their hand-drawn design. All they needed now was a crew. Red called his close friend Hubbard, who had helped out some at Burnside and would certainly second any idea to build something steep and deep in Lincoln City. He also recruited Stefan Hauser, another Burnside local, who had been trying to get a public park built in nearby Seaside. Kimbrough called Lincoln City local Eric Lee. With a core crew assembled, Red urged them to keep the project under their hats, and he quietly relocated to Lincoln City. Burnside was suddenly without its consummate local. Rumors around Portland held that Red was dead, in jail, or both.

Joined by volunteers—including local skater Tavita Scanlan, who put in hours before and after work and during his vacation from his day job as the bottle boy for a local grocer—the crew broke ground on Fourth of July weekend, completely gutting the existing park. Driven by Red's experience, they designed as they built, testing out hardened sections before voting on how to shape subsequent pours. Geth Noble, who had worked with Dawkins in southern Oregon, and Sage joined the project partway through, working long days for a low to nonexistent wage. Tapping out the initial twenty-eight thousand within a month, Ploger worked on finessing more funds as the crew worked overtime and weekends without pay. Two and a half months and a total of sixty-two thousand dollars later, the skateboarders stepped back to admire their eight-thousand-square-foot sculpture, later branded by *Thrasher* as the Gnarliest Skatepark in America.

It was there in Lincoln City where they first started mumbling about forming a legitimate skatepark-building crew. Hubbard wanted to name the company after his Web site, Grindline, where he was already selling T-shirts. Noble's first choice was Airspeed. Other candidates included Mad 'Crete and, for kicks, Great Cambodian Skateparks. Red's best two cents was Dreamland, a somewhat soft name for a tough crew but appropriate nonetheless—they were, after all, creating massive and tangible monuments out of the daydream sketches on their old high school Pee-Chee folders. The idea moved with them and their sentiments turned more serious as they landed their next park, twenty-eight thousand square feet in Newberg, located about halfway along the road back to Portland, a $620,000 job that Hauser deserves much of the credit for securing. In Newberg, the name game boiled down to Dreamland, and Hubbard began marketing Dreamland Skateparks from his Grindline Web site.

By the time Newberg was well under way, Red and the rest of the paid crew had invited Tavita aboard. Sage stayed on as well. Lee stayed home in Lincoln City. Noble invited his girlfriend, Stephanie Mohler, aboard, which, to some, tainted that testosterone-flooded crossroad between concrete work and skateboarding. Heading home to Seattle on a long skate road trip with his then-wife, Jessica, and their toddler, Sophia, Mike Swim was fresh off a Dawkins park in Medford. He passed through Newberg looking for a new gig, volunteering for three days and impressing everybody with his no-bullshit attitude and exceptional finishing talents, which earned him a unanimous invitation to join the "dream team" on its next park, in Aumsville, Oregon.

To a man, those who created the Aumsville skatepark remember the experience as a shining moment in the Dreamland crew's coming of age. Red, Kimbrough, Hubbard, Hauser, Sage, Scanlan, and Swim worked flawlessly together as great friends with little friction. Swim's memory: "Everybody was hyped, putting in a lot of extra time, doing smaller pours, working well together. Everybody was completely into it." And Scanlan's: "Everybody was living together in a tiny house but getting along. We really clicked in Aums. Everybody was on top of their skills, occupying their special spots along the pour. And it shows." Indeed, Aumsville is seamless and buttery smooth.

But like all things too good to be true, their grand alliance would inevitably crumble. Even before Aumsville, Noble and Mohler (who refused to stop being a woman for the sake of abiding by the largely unspoken "No Chicks!" sentiment) had departed, and they later formed Airspeed. Many parks later (including ones in Redmond, Donald, and Astoria, all in Oregon, plus one in Rattenberg, Austria), Hauser took steps to launch his own Seaside-based PTR (Placed to Ride) park-building company. And Hubbard, in a split marked by high emotions and burnout depressions, would ditch Dreamland altogether to build top-of-the-line parks under his own Grindline name. The incomplete story of why Dreamland lost key crew states that the original group contained too many independent, highly creative people sharing homes and working alongside one another every day for months on end. There were simply too many talented cooks in a cramped kitchen. Another good, but not precise, explanation could be summed up with one word: control. Noble's take: "Everybody wants to be 'the guy.' Red wants to be the guy. Hubbard wants to be the guy. Hauser wants to be the guy. I want to be the guy. Even Stephanie wants to be the guy."

With Hubbard's departure, the split ran deep enough to sever fifteen years of friendship. The end came in a thousand cuts: Red keeping his intensely silent communication skills to himself; Hubbard at the last minute skipping out on the Austria park to build the Sumner and Bainbridge parks near his hometown of Seattle; Red fumbling a Request for Proposal for the $2.5 million park in Louisville, Kentucky; Hubbard recruiting business-keen California transplant Chris Hildebrand—who didn't click at all with Red—and continuing to work with him despite a vote of no confidence from the crew majority. Though their personal

NEXT:
JOSH FALK, BURNSIDE, JULY 2002
PHOTO: © ROBERICKSON

rift has since healed somewhat, Red and Hubbard's professional split became final in the summer of 2002, as Dreamland's full-pipe was taking shape in Hailey and the Grindline crew was putting the finishing touches on a mind-blowing park on Washington's Orcas Island. During one explosive conversation, Hubbard declared: "If Red wants a skatepark war, he'll get one!"

War, it is often said, is hell. But in this case, it promised heaven. Many heavens. Big, flowing heavens smooth as glass, with hundreds of blocks of pool coping and over-vert corners and perfectly proportioned hips and pockets. Heavens where grade-school upstarts could step on a skateboard and, taking on the concrete challenges with a child's capacity for quick learning, become the best skateboarders on the planet. Where veteran skaters could still taste the youthful nervousness brought on by supremely fast and massive lines taunting them from all angles and altitudes. Where everyone could laugh off the throbbing pain of a hard slam by dropping into the next preposterously seamless line. Where anybody could ride without paying, without pads, without restraint. That is the enduring legacy of the movement born under the dark and dirty eastern end of Portland's Burnside Bridge: a long future filled with fast freedom.

BACK IN HAILEY, THE AFTERNOON skating lasted until the long shadows signaled it was time to cool down with a few cold ones. Cans of Pabst Blue Ribbon all around. Red held his beer left-handed, numbing that deep gash between the index finger and palm. The bleeding had long since subsided, but it still looked as if a few stitches would be best for sound healing. Red had work to do and couldn't be slowed down by a lasting flesh wound.

Back at the four-bedroom rental where the crew lived during their three months in Hailey, Red's wife, Danyel, inspected the wound as her nine-year-old daughter, Alex, looked at it and said, "Ew," and their two-year-old son, Madison, the spitting image of his old man (and his old man's old man), stared through dark eyes at his father's ragged meat hook. Danyel urged her husband to get some stitches, but Red wasn't about to fork over a chunk of his paycheck to the emergency room. He compromised, and when Danyel returned from the bathroom with a yard of dental floss and a clean sewing needle, Red stitched up his own hand over the kitchen sink.

It was a classic Red maneuver, exemplary of the attitude and follow-through he'd displayed his whole life: in his parents' backyard, building sketchy half-pipes; in his neighbors' front yards, mowing lawns as a young, self-employed landscaper; under the hoods of his rusty '66 Chevy with the bass-ackward gearbox and of his wife's long-gone '88, which survived most of an interstate road trip after he had bypassed a broken engine belt bracket with baling wire and a bungee cord; and in the eastern pit under Portland's Burnside Bridge, where his do-it-yourself approach infected an entire generation of skateboarders who had little choice but to build their own scene.

IF YOU DON'T LEARN THE HARD WAY, YOU' AIN'T SHIT

MARK "RED" SCOTT

LONGTIME BURNSIDE LOCAL LITTLE JON NURSING A HEAD INJURY

PHOTO COURTESY OF DANYEL SCOTT

IN THE EARLY '90S, *DÉSIRÉE ASTORGA* DITCHED THE STOCK MARKET FOR A LIFE OF SNOWBOARDING AND SKATEBOARDING. SHE STARTED SHOOTING SOON THEREAFTER, WENT FULL-TIME IN 1999, AND NOW CONTRIBUTES TO SEVERAL SKATEBOARDING AND SURFING MAGAZINES. OTHER CLIENTS INCLUDE VANS AND ROXY.
GET HOLD OF HER AT WWW.HOMEPAGE.MAC.COM/DESIREERASTORGA

DAVE BJORN HAS BEEN LIVING AND SHOOTING PICTURES ON THE ISLANDS OF HAWAII SINCE 1978. "IT'S BEEN A KILLER RIDE," HE SAYS, "AND I THANK JESUS FOR IT."
CONTACT HIM AT BJORN@HAWAII.RR.COM

MICHAEL BREAM HAS BEEN PURSUING PHOTOGRAPHY AS A HOBBY SINCE HE WAS A KID. IN 1994, HE FOUNDED GRAVITY SKATEBOARDS, BASED IN NORTH SAN DIEGO COUNTY.
CHECK IT OUT AT WWW.GRAVITYBOARD.COM

FOUNDING PHOTO EDITOR OF *TRANSWORLD SKATEBOARDING* MAGAZINE AND CURRENT DIRECTOR OF PHOTOGRAPHY FOR *THE SKATEBOARD MAG*, *J. GRANT BRITTAIN* STARTED PHOTOGRAPHING SKATEBOARDERS WHILE MANAGING DEL MAR SKATE RANCH IN THE EARLY '80S. ONE OF THE MOST RESPECTED LENSMEN IN SKATEBOARDING, HE HAS TRAINED SOME OF TODAY'S BEST SKATE PHOTOGRAPHERS. HIS PORTFOLIO ALSO INCLUDES ABSTRACTS, PORTRAITS, LANDSCAPES, AND TRAVEL.
GIVE IT A LOOK AT WWW.JGRANTBRITTAIN.COM

KENT DAHLGREN USED TO TAKE A NICE CAMERA DOWN TO BURNSIDE SKATEPARK UNTIL IT GOT DROPPED AND RUN OVER AND SMASHED. HE REPLACED IT WITH A DISPOSABLE, WITH WHICH HE CAPTURED MUCH OF THE PROJECT'S FORMATIVE YEARS.
HE LIVES OUTSIDE PORTLAND, OREGON, AND IS NOT A PHOTOGRAPHER

BORN AND RAISED IN SANTA CRUZ, CALIFORNIA, *DAN DEVINE* STARTED SURFING IN 1968 AND GOT HIS FIRST SHOT PUBLISHED IN *SURFER* TWO YEARS LATER. IN THE EARLY '70S, HE STARTED PHOTOGRAPHING SKATEBOARDERS. HE HAS LIVED AND SURFED AND SHOT IN HAWAII FOR THE PAST SIXTEEN YEARS.

NEW YORK–BASED *ROB ERICKSON* HAS BEEN SKATEBOARDING AND SHOOTING PICTURES OF SKATEBOARDERS FOR ABOUT TWENTY YEARS. HE ALSO LIKES SHOOTING BANDS. HIS IMAGES CAN BE FOUND IN *BIG BROTHER*, *SLAP*, AND *THRASHER*,
AND HE ALSO BUILDS EXCEPTIONAL WEB SITES, INCLUDING HIS OWN, WWW.ROBERICKSON.COM

CONTRIBUTING PHOTOGRAPHERS

MOST OF *GLEN E. FRIEDMAN*'S SEMINAL IMAGES ARE COLLECTED IN HIS FOUR SELF-PUBLISHED BOOKS: *FUCK YOU HEROES, FUCK YOU TOO, THE IDEALIST,* AND *DOGTOWN: THE LEGEND OF THE Z-BOYS.*
FOR MORE INFO, CHECK OUT WWW.BURNINGFLAGS.COM

JOURNEYMAN SHOOTER *CHRISTOPHER GARDNER* STUDIED AT THE BROOKS INSTITUTE OF PHOTOGRAPHY IN SANTA BARBARA BEFORE LAUNCHING HIS PROFESSIONAL CAREER IN 1986. HE'S CURRENTLY A STAFF PHOTOGRAPHER FOR THE NEW TIMES MEDIA GROUP IN SAN LUIS OBISPO, CALIFORNIA.
REACH HIM AT FOTOGOGO@YAHOO.COM

SAN FRANCISCO–BASED *ERIC GONZALES* HAS BEEN SKATEBOARDING SINCE 1986 AND SHOOTING SINCE 1991. HIS IMAGES CAN BE SEEN IN *CONCUSSION, THRASHER, SKRATCH,* AND AT WWW.LIBERATIONMEDIA.COM. HE ALSO PLAYS GUITAR FOR THE ANGRY AMPUTEES.
CHECK THEIR TOUR DATES AT WWW.ANGRYAMPUTEES.COM

RETIRED WRITER, EDITOR, AND PHOTOGRAPHER *JAMES GREGORY* FIRST APPEARED IN *WHO'S WHO IN THE WORLD* IN 2001. HE LIVES IN GLENDALE, CALIFORNIA, AND IS FILMING A SEQUEL TO *MIRACLE ON 34TH STREET.*

PORTLAND, OREGON–BASED *JOE HAMMEKE* IS A STAFF PHOTOGRAPHER FOR *THRASHER.* HE SAYS HE LOVES SKATING BURNSIDE AND ALL THE DREAMLAND AND GRINDLINE SKATEPARKS THROUGHOUT THE PACIFIC NORTHWEST AND ACROSS THE PLANET, AND SPENDS THE REST OF HIS TIME PHOTOGRAPHING STREET SKATERS WHEN IT'S NOT RAINING AND SOMETIMES WHEN IT IS.
REACH HIM AT JOEHAMMEKE@HOTMAIL.COM

GRADUATING FROM UC IN 2003 WITH A DEGREE IN VISUAL ARTS, *SARAH HARRON* HAS DOCUMENTED MUCH OF THE BACKBREAKING CONCRETE WORK GOING DOWN UNDER THE BRIDGE OVER WASHINGTON STREET.
SHE LIVES IN SAN DIEGO WITH INDY THE DINGO

JON HUMPHRIES GREW UP SKATING IN THE PACIFIC NORTHWEST AND GOT INTO PHOTOGRAPHY IN 1992. HE WAS A STAFFER AT *TRANSWORLD SKATEBOARDING* FROM 1997 TO 2003. HIS WEB SITE, WWW.JONHUMPHRIESPHOTO.COM, SHOULD BE UP BY NOW.
IF NOT, WRITE HIM AT HUMPHRIESPHOTO@HOTMAIL.COM

THE SKATEBOARD MAG STAFF PHOTOGRAPHER *ATIBA JEFFERSON* STARTED SKATEBOARDING IN 1990 AND GOT INTO PHOTOGRAPHY THREE YEARS LATER.
HE LIVES IN HOLLYWOOD AND CAN BE REACHED THROUGH WWW.ATIBAPHOTO.COM

CHRIS KARDAS'S SKATEBOARD PHOTO ARCHIVE STRETCHES BACK INTO THE '80S, AND HE'S BEEN SHOOTING SNOWBOARDING ALMOST AS LONG.
HE WAS LAST SPOTTED IN OREGON

GROWING UP IN ALHAMBRA, CALIFORNIA, *STEVE KEENAN* STARTED SHOOTING SKATE PHOTOS IN 1979. HE CONTRIBUTED TO *THRASHER* AND *TRANSWORLD* IN THE EARLY '80S AND WORKED FROM 1986 TO 1991 AS A STAFF PHOTOGRAPHER AND VIDEOGRAPHER FOR SANTA CRUZ SKATEBOARDS. HE COFOUNDED CONSOLIDATED SKATEBOARDS IN 1991 AND HELPED RUN IT UNTIL 1997. HE'S BEEN SKATING SINCE 1969 AND LIVES IN SANTA CRUZ.
JASON JESSEE KNOWS HOW TO GET HOLD OF HIM

LAURA KLEINHENZ DOESN'T SKATE, BUT HER PHOTOGRAPHS HAVE APPEARED IN *TIME, NEWSWEEK,* AND THE *NEW YORK TIMES.* SHE'S ALSO A KICK-ASS WEDDING PHOTOGRAPHER.
CHECK OUT HER DOCUMENTARY PROJECTS AT WWW.LAURAKLEINHENZ.COM. SHE LIVES IN LOS ANGELES WITH HER DOG, DORY

JIM KNIGHT GREW UP IN BAKERSFIELD, CALIFORNIA, AND STARTED SKATEBOARDING IN 1976. A YEAR LATER, HE STARTED SHOOTING SKATE PHOTOS OF HIS FRIENDS WITH A HAND-ME-DOWN THIRTY-FIVE-MILLIMETER ARGUS FROM HIS DAD. HE TOOK PHOTOGRAPHY CLASSES IN HIGH SCHOOL AND THEN AT THE CITY COLLEGE IN SANTA BARBARA, WHERE HE LANDED A JOB AT POWELL-PERALTA AS AN OFFICIAL BONES BRIGADE PHOTOGRAPHER. HE'S BEEN WORKING FOR POWELL SINCE 1987 AND STILL SKATES AND TAKES LOTS OF PICTURES OF HIS FRIENDS.

OCCASIONALLY CONTRIBUTING TO *THRASHER* AND *CONCUSSION, CHARLIE MIDDLETON* HAS BEEN SHOOTING AS A HOBBY FOR OVER A DECADE.
HE'S A WELDER AND LIVES IN SAN DIEGO

SUPER-8 ENTHUSIAST *PAT MYERS* ENJOYS SHOOTING PRETTY PICTURES OF UGLY SKATERS, MOSTLY FOR *JUICE* AND *THRASHER.* OTHER CLIENTS INCLUDE QUICKSILVER, BLACK LABEL, 1984, AND DESTRUCTO.
A HAWAII NATIVE BASED IN NEWPORT BEACH, HE CAN BE REACHED AT P@TMYERS.ORG

JIM O'MAHONEY, WHO SAYS HE GOT THE WORD *SKATEBOARD* PUT IN THE DICTIONARY, ORGANIZED MANY OF SKATEBOARDING'S BIG EVENTS DURING THE '70S.
THESE DAYS, WHEN HE'S NOT RIDING SKATER'S POINT SKATEPARK, HE'S THE CURATOR OF THE SANTA BARBARA SURFING MUSEUM

SKATEBOARDER MAGAZINE STAFFER *MICHAEL O'MEALLY* WAS BORN AND RAISED IN SYDNEY, AUSTRALIA, AND STARTED RIDING IN 1982. A DECADE LATER DURING A COLLEGE ELECTIVE, HE STARTED SHOOTING PHOTOGRAPHS OF HIS FRIENDS SKATING. THE LECTURER TOLD HIM HE'D NEVER GET ANYWHERE AS A SKATEBOARD PHOTOGRAPHER. SOON THEREAFTER, HE STARTED SHOOTING FOR *SLAM* MAGAZINE, BEFORE LIVING IN NEW YORK CITY, WHERE HE SHOT FOR *SLAP* AND *THRASHER.* WHEN HE'S NOT LAPPING THE PLANET TO DOCUMENT SKATEBOARDING, HE HANGS HIS HAT IN LOS ANGELES.
GET HOLD OF HIM AT MICHAELOMEALLY@HOTMAIL.COM

MASSACHUSETTS-BORN *CHRIS "RHINO" ROONEY* HAS BEEN SKATEBOARDING SINCE 1976 AND SHOOTING PROFESSIONALLY SINCE 1997. HIS WORK APPEARS FREQUENTLY IN *THRASHER* AND MANY OTHER SKATEBOARDING MAGAZINES.
HE LIVES IN SAN DIEGO AND CAN BE REACHED AT RHINO4366@AOL.COM

SCOTT STARR, 1988 WORLD AMATEUR FREESTYLE FRISBEE CHAMPION, HAS BEEN SHOOTING SKATEBOARDING, SURFING, AND SNOWBOARDING SINCE 1982. HE WAS A PHOTOGRAPHER FOR *THRASHER* FROM 1988 THROUGH THE MID-'90S, AND HIS WORK HAS ALSO APPEARED IN *SURFER'S JOURNAL, CONCRETE WAVE,* AND OTHERS.
HE LIVES IN SANTA BARBARA AND CAN BE REACHED AT STARR.PHOTO@GTE.NET

NEW YORK–BASED *GERHARD STOCHL* HAS PHOTOGRAPHED SKATEBOARDERS ALL OVER THE WORLD. HIS IMAGES HAVE BEEN PUBLISHED IN MOST OF THE FINER SKATEBOARD MAGAZINES, AND HE'S ALSO SHOT FOR *SOMA, ANTHEM, LODOWN,* AND *INDEX,* AS WELL AS NIKE, ZOO YORK, AND CARHARTT EUROPE.
FOR MORE INFO, GO TO WWW.STOCHLFOTO.COM

TED TERREBONE STARTED SKATEBOARDING IN 1962 IN CARSON CITY, NEVADA. IN THE MID-'70S, HE TAUGHT HIMSELF PHOTOGRAPHY BASICS BEFORE ENROLLING IN A CLASS AT THE UNIVERSITY OF NEVADA, RENO. IN 1977, HIS FIRST PUBLISHED SHOT RAN IN *SKATEBOARDER,* WHERE HE EVENTUALLY BECAME A STAFFER. HE RUNS A PRINT SHOP IN THE BAY AREA AND SHOOTS ON THE WEEKENDS MOSTLY, CONTRIBUTING TO *JUICE.*
CHECK OUT T BONE PHOTO: WWW.GEOCITIES.COM/TBONEPHOTO/

MARK WATERS GREW UP IN SAN JOSE, CALIFORNIA, WHERE HE STARTED SKATEBOARDING IN THE EARLY '70S. HE DISCOVERED PUNK ROCK IN THE EARLY '80S AND BEGAN SHOOTING PHOTOS SOON THEREAFTER, FOCUSING ON BOTH OF HIS PASSIONS, AND HASN'T STOPPED SINCE.
SAMPLES OF HIS WORK ARE ON HIS WEB SITE, WWW.SKATEPUNK.COM

JAY WESTCOTT HAS BEEN SHOOTING OFF AND ON SINCE 1995. HE CONTRIBUTES TO *JUICE* AND *TRUCKSTOP* AND WORKS FOR *THE JOURNAL* NEWSPAPERS. HE LIVES IN WOODBRIDGE, VIRGINIA, WITH HIS WIFE AND LITTLE GIRL.
CHECK OUT HIS WORK AT WWW.JAYWESTCOTT.COM